FORDNATION

FORD NATION

TWO BROTHERS, ONE VISION

ROB FORD & DOUG FORD

HarperCollins*PublishersLtd*

Ford Nation

Published by HarperCollins Publishers Ltd

First published by HarperCollins Publishers in a hardcover edition: 2016
This trade paperback edition: 2018

Unless otherwise noted, all photographs in the book are courtesy of the authors.

The authors gratefully acknowledge Postmedia, *National Post* and the *Toronto Sun* for the use of their photographs in this book.

Eulogies for Rob Ford by Mike Del Grande, Clinton Leonard, Gavin Tighe and Stephanie Ford are reprinted with their permission.

The Rex Murphy eulogy for Rob Ford is reproduced with the permission of Rex Murphy/CBC Licensing.

The Rob Ford quotations from an interview on *The Bill Carroll Show* that aired October 1, 2015, are reproduced with the permission of Corus Radio Toronto.

HarperCollins books may be purchased for educational, business, or sales promotional use through our Special Markets Department.

HarperCollins Publishers Ltd
Bay Adelaide Centre, East Tower
22 Adelaide Street West, 41st Floor
Toronto, Ontario
M5H 4E3

www.harpercollins.ca

Canadian Cataloguing in Publication information is available upon request.

ISBN 978-1-44345-176-5

Printed and bound in the United States of America
LSC/H 10 9 8 7 6 5 4 3 2 1

To our mom and dad, who were always there for us,
and to all the people of Ford Nation, who
believed in Rob no matter what.

CONTENTS

CHAPTER 1 The Most Misunderstood Mayor in the World 1
CHAPTER 2 The Ford Family 15
CHAPTER 3 Doug and Diane 31
CHAPTER 4 Deco 39
CHAPTER 5 Entering the Fray 45
CHAPTER 6 Dad Leads the Way 53
CHAPTER 7 Lessons from Our Father 59
CHAPTER 8 A Man of the People 65
CHAPTER 9 Rob's First Years 73
CHAPTER 10 Second Term 77
CHAPTER 11 Doug 87
CHAPTER 12 Chicago Calling 97
CHAPTER 13 The Once and Future Mayor 103
CHAPTER 14 Last Stop: Gravy Train 123
CHAPTER 15 Selling Toronto to the World 147
CHAPTER 16 The Silent Majority 163
CHAPTER 17 Under Fire 167
CHAPTER 18 Roller Coaster Ride 177
CHAPTER 19 Late-Breaking News 195
CHAPTER 20 Infamy 203
CHAPTER 21 Getting Help 217
CHAPTER 22 The Diagnosis 235
CHAPTER 23 Saying Goodbye 251
CHAPTER 24 Looking Forward 271
Endnotes 281

FORDNATION

CHAPTER 1

The Most Misunderstood Mayor in the World

You never beat cancer, that's one thing. There's no new tumours, that's great . . . [If] I had to do this for the rest of my life, I have no problem doing it. The alternative, I don't want to be pushing up tulips in the next few years, which I could have been doing. I would have been dead by now. Something has happened for a reason, and I want to thank whoever, my dad, or the good Lord, for making this happen. It might sound crazy to you, but I can't thank people enough for their support.[1]

—Rob Ford, in an interview on AM640's *Bill Carroll Show*, October 1, 2015

Election night for the Toronto 2010 municipal election was held on October 25. It would make a good story to say it was a nail-biter, but it really wasn't. Rob Ford, my younger brother, was announced as the winner almost immediately—not much more than six minutes into the ballot counting. Rob had won the election with almost 400,000 votes. The next closest was the downtown left-wing favourite, "Furious" George Smitherman, at 289,000. Voter turnout that year was over 50 percent, the highest the city had seen in a long time.

Rob's campaign had been a roller coaster ride from the start, and we'd had lots of opportunities to worry about his prospects; Rob's no-bullshit attitude and dedication to fiscal responsibility had already made him unpopular with a lot of the elites. But we also had no idea that he was leading a surge of populist solidarity—regular people who, regardless of the way they'd voted in the past, were sick of lacklustre politics as usual. With Rob's victory, these people had spoken.

Rob was inaugurated in early December. Don Cherry, of course, was a huge highlight at Rob's inauguration ceremony. Don was a big supporter of Rob's. I believe they'd gotten to know each other after Don listened to Rob on AM640. Rob's views weren't too far off Don's own opinions. Anyone who's ever watched *Coach's Corner* knows that Don is a pretty direct, tell-it-like-it-is kind of guy, so we decided that we were going to have him come and put the chain of office around Rob's neck.

Although his speech was meant to be funny and lighthearted, Don still had some important things to say, especially when he related a story about how Rob helped an older woman get reimbursed (to the tune of $5,000, no less) after the city cut down a century-old tree in her yard . . . and then stuck her with the bill. Cherry concluded by saying, "And that's why I say he's going to be the greatest mayor this city has ever seen, as far as I'm concerned, and put that in your pipe, you left-wing kooks. Thank you very much."[2]

Naturally, a bunch of the left-leaning councillors in the crowd were pissed off about Cherry's speech. Some of them even turned their chairs around and showed their backs when Don was speaking—but many of the same people were in line to get his autograph after the TV cameras were off. (Looking back on it now, that was a symbol of all the craziness to come over the next few years.)

After Cherry's speech, Rob gave his own remarks. He congratulated each councillor on being elected and told everyone that it feels great to help people.[3] In my opinion, he came across as humble. In fact, as I listened to my brother, I felt that his inauguration speech kind of showed his natural shyness. That shyness was a side of Rob not many people understood.

I'd just been voted in as councillor of Ward 2, Etobicoke North, Rob's old seat. For my part, I'd never been more proud of Rob, and with the campaigning and election behind us—not to mention the most memorable inauguration in Toronto's history—it was time to get to work.

But just as we hadn't predicted the populism that had brought Rob to victory, we also didn't know the extent of the opposition already lining up against him. This opposition included political rivals and a relentless media, who were intent on ensuring that Rob's every move would be shown in the spotlight.

FAST FORWARD TO August 11, 2016—almost six months after Rob succumbed to cancer. The publication ban was lifted on the so-called crack video that had sidelined the last year of his mayoralty and revealed an alcohol addiction that eventually led him to rehab. The crack video isn't very long, not much more than a minute. It shows my brother in an obviously impaired state and, yes, he smokes something out of a pipe. I'm not making excuses for what Rob is shown to do in the video, or the things he's pressed into saying while impaired. But my question is, what's the point of releasing this video? Rob is gone, but much of the media *still* seems to have it out for him.

When the video was made public, my first reaction was one of utter disgust. Rob's immediate family—his wife, Renata, and his children, Stephanie and Dougie—are still reeling from his death at age 46. This video has kicked them while they're already down. But the impact on Rob's family has never seemed of much concern to the mainstream media. From the day Rob announced his plan to run for mayor of Toronto, the media descended like vultures.

And the spotlight wasn't just confined to Rob, Renata and their kids; it was also turned on my wife and daughters, as well as our mother and other siblings. We had a steady stream of journalists at our homes in Etobicoke, at our family cottage, at our places of work. Our feeling was that the media—predominantly the left-wing outlets such as the *Star* and *The Globe and Mail*—were waiting for any crumb of news, no matter how tiny (or how irrelevant, as in the case of the video released after the person in it had died), which they could use to take down a non-establishment political figure like Rob. When I think about it that way, I guess it's no surprise that our family was treated like collateral damage. Never in Canadian politics has the mainstream media had a vendetta against someone to the extent they did against my brother.

Rob and I sat down and started to work on this book in the winter of 2016. Unfortunately, his health declined soon thereafter and he wasn't able to participate in the book the way we had planned. I spoke to him about the book more than once before he passed away, and he insisted that we complete it if he wasn't around to do so. He was too sick to do any interviews for the book, as he needed all his strength for the various treatments, and then he became so sick that there was no longer any question about his participating further in the book at all. His family came first, as it always had.

After Rob died and the funeral was over and everything calmed down a bit, I talked to the family about the book, and we agreed that, as Rob had wanted, we would finish it. We decided we wouldn't put words in Rob's mouth. Instead, we decided to let Rob speak for himself, drawing on various press conferences and interviews he's done over the years. You'll read Rob's own words throughout the book, his opinions and perspectives, as I tell the story of Rob, me and our family, and what really happened. This is as much Rob's book as it is mine. We are partners on this book—co-authors—as we were in life. We are also fortunate to have additional remarks from our mother, Diane, our nephew Michael, and Rob's wife, Renata. I believe their commentary adds balance to mine and also reveals more about Rob Ford the person.

I know our family has been described (some might say accused) as highly political, as if we've always had some kind of secret long-term plan. But that isn't it. We were never into secret plans or backroom strategy at all. My dad—the first Ford to hold political office—just didn't operate that way, and Rob and I took our example from him. The first time I heard us called the "Canadian Kennedys," I got ticked off. We never had anything in common with a family like that. But then I had to laugh about it, because it was such bullshit. We just represent the people, and that's it. We're about as grassroots as they come. That was a bit of a problem with Rob, actually. Sometimes he was too average and grassroots; he would forget he was mayor and get himself too involved in the problems he was trying to fix. In any case, there's never been a vault in the house on Weston Wood Road where we keep the top secret Ford-family strategic plan.

If there is a Ford family plan, there's nothing secret about it, and—when it comes to running things at the municipal level—it's just four simple principles. The first is customer service excellence. Return every single phone call or, better yet, show up at the caller's door. That doesn't happen with the majority of politicians. They send their assistants, or their assistants answer the phone, and nothing much happens after that. The second principle is reduce the size and cost of government. We know there's tons of waste. But there are also tons of efficiencies that can be implemented, and people don't have to be laid off. The third principle is make government transparent and accountable. Getting rid of the sole-source deals is a good way to start, but the main thing is making sure all the politicians aren't on the gravy train, spending tens of thousands of dollars on free trips, and going all over the place. The final principle is rapid underground transit, or, in Rob's own words, "Subways, subways, subways." It's as simple as that.

I firmly believe that Rob's mayoralty was an unprecedented success, despite the scandals. For starters, in the four years of Rob's administration, the city of Toronto took significant strides forward and got to a place where it was working more efficiently than ever before. That was due in large part to Rob's simple but effective devotion to customer service. He and I had both learned customer service from our dad, Doug Ford Sr; at its most basic level, it just meant being accessible, honest and fair with people's money. That had served us well at Deco Labels and Tags, our family business, and it served us even better in our political careers. But as mayor, Rob took customer service excellence to an unprecedented level. Nowhere was this more apparent than in the top-to-bottom transformational changes made to the Toronto Transit Commission. Most notably, Rob made the TTC an essential service, which meant that riders—the customers, in this case—were protected from transit strikes like the ones that had crippled other large regions throughout the province.

Rob also devoted his administration to running an open, transparent and accountable municipal government. He achieved this through renewing public faith in the long-troubled Toronto Community Housing Corporation, by making the attendance records of city councillors available online and, most notably, by posting the expenses of councillors, committees and senior managers. For the first time, the taxpayers of Toronto could see who was expensing what—and hold them accountable for it.

Under Rob's watch, the size and cost of government was reduced. Hundreds of millions of dollars in efficiencies were found, with minimal impact on front-line services (except for a brief librarians' strike), less money was spent the first year than in the previous, there was a zero-percent tax increase, and we had the lowest property tax of any large city in North America. Toronto was ranked one of the top cities in the world to work in, and among the top cities in the world to live in (although I personally believe that Toronto is number one). The much-hated personal vehicle tax was eliminated. The mayor's budget was reduced by $700,000, while councillor expense budgets were reduced to $30,000. Garbage collection west of Yonge Street was contracted out, which saved millions of dollars and eliminated the risk of future public-sector garbage strikes in west Toronto. Rob's approach to budgeting moved the city into long-term fiscal sustainability and stopped out-of-control spending. He negotiated historic labour deals and collective agreements with the city's unions that both improved efficiency and saved hundreds of millions of dollars—without a single day of labour disruption.

Rob devised a bold vision for improved transportation and transit across the entire city, starting with a plan to extend the Bloor-Danforth subway much farther into Scarborough. Rob believed that the TTC is the backbone of Toronto and that a strategic investment was needed to build a world-class transit system. To this end, he negotiated a historic deal with the provincial and federal levels of government to help bear the costs of the subway extension; by the time Rob's term was finished, his successor would only need to hit the "on" switch to execute this transit plan. As far as surface transportation went, Rob saw to it that hundreds of kilometres of streets were resurfaced and close to 200,000 potholes were filled every year. (Potholes were near and dear to Rob's heart, which I will talk about later on.)

These accomplishments speak for themselves—not that the media has been particularly interested in them—but the heart of Rob's political success was simply taking care of people, which he demonstrated by returning their calls or knocking on their doors. In his own words, he loved "[taking] care of people that have never been taken care of before. The poorest people. I'll go right to their front door. As you know, I've spent a lot of time, I've spent probably 70 to 80 percent of my time in Toronto community housing, knocking on doors in the toughest neighbourhoods like Jane and Finch, Malvern, Scarborough . . . I've helped out these families, and I guess the word gets around: you call Rob Ford, as of this day, I'll still return your call personally, and I'll come to your front door to serve you . . . I return probably close to 25, 30 calls a day, easy."[4]

That was my brother's true passion: helping people out, regardless of their political stripe. At the same time, he had his demons. The biggest of those demons wasn't crack, as the infamous video seems to suggest. Rob's biggest demon, plain and simple, was alcohol. Close to the end, in his interview with Bill Carroll, Rob described it best: "I'm an alcoholic. I can't have one drink. It's like I have to have 100 or none . . . When you're in that sort of shape, or you're in that sort of mindset, you're really lonely, and you'll really hang on to anyone that will watch you do, or listen to what you have to say, and it's anyone at that time. It's just excuses. I'm not using excuses, I'm just being real with you. I just let a lot of people down. I've got thousands and thousands of hours and days and months to try to gain people's respect back, and maybe I've lost some forever . . ."[5]

It took Rob a long time to acknowledge the extent of his addiction. And it took me just as long to acknowledge what was happening to him. Maybe I could've intervened earlier. I don't know. All I do know is that his many successes, his devotion to helping people, and by extension our whole family, have been bulldozed by a mainstream media intent on depicting Rob as a drug-fuelled, out-of-control monster. I'll do my best to show the good person he truly was. Flawed, yes, and struggling with alcoholism, but a good person nonetheless.

Not long ago, I had a dream about Rob. I'm sure it wasn't more than 10 seconds long, although it felt much longer. Anyway, in the dream there he was, as real as if he was still alive and in the room today. The feeling stayed with me when I woke up; I was happy through the rest of the morning. Personally, I don't know what happens after death. People all have their different beliefs. I'm a strong believer in God. I guess, someday, we'll all find out what happens when we die. Maybe I'll see him again after all.

The funny thing is, Rob always said he was going to die young. I don't know what his spiritual or religious beliefs were, really. That wasn't the kind of conversation we ever got into. But whatever he believed, he often told me, "I'm gonna kick the bucket early, Jones." That was even well before he knew he had cancer—he just seemed sure of it. I often think of how he was larger than life when he was alive. He's even bigger, it seems, now that he's gone. Anywhere I go, every event I attend, people talk to me about him. He's become a legend. I just wish we'd had a little more time together. A month, a week, a day, anything.

The family and I hope you enjoy the book and seeing the human side of Rob that the media never properly shared. We miss him dearly, and we are grateful that you have taken the opportunity to read about the real Rob Ford.

Thanks for everything, Jones.

CHAPTER 2

The Ford Family

When you meet one Ford, you meet and know them all. So while Rob's dad, Doug Sr, was the first [Ford] I met as a member of our Common Sense Revolution caucus in 1995, the others soon followed. And as the late Jim Flaherty and I found out, when you were a friend of one Ford, you were a friend of them all, and they with you. Politics is hardest on the people who don't run for office. It's hardest for those who love us at home. The public scrutiny, the interrupted dinners, the late nights and the busy weekends all take their toll on our families. But the Ford family seems to thrive on their contributions to public service.[1]

—MIKE HARRIS, FORMER PREMIER OF ONTARIO

It was a day in mid-spring—May 28, 1969. I was four and a half years old, and I distinctly remember standing with my dad on the grounds outside Humber Memorial Hospital in north Etobicoke.

"Look up," my dad told me, pointing to the windows

of the third floor. "That's where your mom is, and that's where your new brother is being born."

To this day, I'm not sure why we weren't inside the hospital, but my memory of standing outside with my dad is crystal clear. Until that point, I'd been the youngest of the Ford kids. My sister, Kathy, was the eldest, having been born in 1960. Then in 1962, my brother Randy was born. I came along on November 20, 1964. And five years later, here was Rob. Nobody could've imagined the life he was going to lead, or the lasting impact he would have on the city he loved so much. It was another few days before Mom and Rob were able to come home from the hospital, and by then it had started to really sink in: I had a little brother. I was pretty young myself, but I remember understanding right from day one that it was my job to take care of him, protect him and help him out. Maybe it was instinct, but it was a feeling that never went away.

I still feel that way, even with him gone.

In spite of the five years between us, Rob and I were always as close as two brothers can be. Our older siblings, Kathy and Randy, got along well with each other. They were closer in age, only 18 months apart, so it kind of evolved into the two younger ones—Rob and me—versus the two older ones, but overall we all looked out for each other. As a kid, I had a paper route, delivering *The Globe and Mail*, which Rob helped me out with. We'd wake up at five in the morning to deliver the papers. With some of the money I earned from the paper route, I would buy him hockey cards. He loved collecting those cards; it was part of how much he loved the game in general. As he grew up, the only sport he came to love more than hockey was football. Both games were a big part of shaping who he was, and I can't imagine my brother's life without sports in it.

Rob's first school was Westmount Junior School, on Chapman Road in Etobicoke. On one very hot day when Rob was in kindergarten, he and two friends decided to walk home at recess. Naturally, a big panic followed when recess ended and three kids were missing, but sure enough, Rob and his friends arrived home completely fine. I don't think there was ever any real danger; Etobicoke was a very safe neighbourhood back then (it still is, if you ask me), but just imagine how much panic there would be nowadays if three little kids disappeared from kindergarten at recess.

One time when he was still quite young, Rob told us he wanted to move to Scarlettwood Court. This was a community housing project, consisting mostly of low-rises and townhouses, off Scarlett Road on the west side of the Humber River. Back when Rob was a kid, everyone at Scarlettwood Court knew everyone else. They all grew up together, and they were certainly as welcome on our street as we were on theirs. Anyway, Scarlettwood Court was where a number of Rob's friends lived, and I remember him coming to my parents and saying, "Can we move to Scarlettwood Court?"

Rob wasn't older than six or seven. My parents thought it was cute, and just said okay. They thought it was interesting how Rob's mind worked—how he'd rather be with his friends in community housing than in the home our dad had had custom-built for us.

But maybe, for Rob, Scarlettwood Court and the friends he had there were the roots of his dedication to the Toronto Community Housing Corporation (TCHC). The TCHC was formed in 2002 as an amalgamation of a number of pre-existing affordable housing providers. Especially as a councillor, Rob was passionate about serving TCHC residents. He made a point of visiting TCHC buildings as often as he could. Some of the conditions he found were deplorable. There were bed bugs, cockroaches, mice, holes in the walls, broken appliances, among many other problems. Rob would walk through the buildings with the TCHC representatives in tow. He would knock on every single door and ask the residents what their problems were, and then he would turn around to the TCHC rep and say, "Get it done." And after his visits, mattresses would get replaced, holes in walls would get patched, new appliances would be brought in. In other words, he made a real difference.

A lot of politicians, particularly those on the left, seem to like to talk about people living in community housing or similar situations. Rob and I thought of these kinds of politicians as "poverty pimps," because for all their talk, they never actually seemed to do much. It was as if poverty-pimp politicians were happy to just use the folks in community housing as a convenient backdrop or talking point and leave it at that. Not Rob, though. He wasn't doing those visits just to talk. He was there to get things done, because he truly knew those people.

That's not to say Rob didn't believe in working hard and being self-reliant to get yourself out of a tough financial situation. He absolutely believed in that philosophy. He just happened to have a big heart—and some real understanding—to go along with it.

A lot of Etobicoke was still farmland in the late 1960s and early 1970s. In fact, there was a pony farm at the corner of Kipling and Eglinton. You could visit the farm on weekends and ride the ponies, but on our birthdays, my dad would rent a pony and bring it to our backyard. At one of Rob's early birthdays, the pony took off. It was trying to get back to its stable, I guess. I remember how my dad had to run down the street, chasing it. That was a good hike from The Westway and Kipling up to Eglinton and Kipling, trying to chase a pony. Good thing the traffic then wasn't nearly as crazy as it is now.

My dad wasn't a big sports fan—not like Rob and me—but in 1972, when Canada was playing the Russians in the Summit Series, Dad had a whole bunch of Team Canada stickers printed off at work. We plastered the stickers all over our family Plymouth. Dad had even gotten official permission to print the stickers from an acquaintance of his, a guy named Al Eagleson, who'd been one of the organizers of the Summit Series. Dad had volunteered on Eagleson's campaign to run as a provincial Tory back in 1963. Anyway, Al Eagleson really made his name as one of the biggest figures in professional hockey management. Unfortunately, he went on to end up in quite a bit of legal trouble in the 1990s, but back in the early 1970s, he was a well-respected figure in both provincial politics and professional sports.

Outside of the Summit Series, Rob and I were big fans of the Maple Leafs, of course. And since Weston Wood was a dead-end street, we could play road hockey all the time. On the weekends and in the summer, we'd play from morning until the street lights came on. Rob started playing hockey over at Centennial Park Arena when he was six years old. I'd already been playing for a couple of years at that point. Our games were usually three hours apart on Saturday mornings, so we'd stay there to watch other teams play as well. If Rob scored a goal during a game, we'd go to McDonald's afterwards for milkshakes.

As we got older, Rob and I actually got the chance to play hockey together. This came later, when I was in my early 20s. I was playing industrial league up at Chesswood and Westwood Arenas. My team was in the A Division, where there were a lot of Junior A and Junior B players who couldn't go any further in their careers but still wanted to play good hockey. The industrial league was very competitive but a lot of fun as well. Even though he was only 16—younger than the rest of us—my team took Rob on because he was a tough, good player. (For the record, if Rob was still here today, he'd say he was the better player, but it's not true—*I* was always the better player!) Anyway, we both played forward, and in one of Rob's very first games, a couple of guys from the other team took a run at him. Well, I was after both of them in two seconds flat, and from then on, I became known as Rob's protector. Even after they separated us on the line, I'd jump over the boards and go after anyone else that took a run at him. I didn't always need to—Rob could hold his own against anyone—but he was my little brother. What else was I supposed to do?

I loved being Rob's big brother. When I was working at Canada Packers in the summers of my teenage years, I'd come home late at night after my shift to find the upper floors of our house almost unbearably hot. We rarely used the air conditioning in the house, and one of the only fans was in Rob's room. Rob was probably 10 or 11 at this time. I would creep into his room, unplug the fan and bring it back to my room. Then, once I had it going, I could count one minute—even a bit less—before Rob would come along with his blanket and his pillow, half asleep, and lie down on a mattress on the floor beside my bed. I used some of my earnings from Canada Packers to buy him a new pair of skates for hockey. I always felt like he looked up to me. He was proud when he came to watch me play football or hockey. It was no different when the two of us were at city hall together. Rob was working hard to do the right thing, and I never stopped looking out for him.

Rob discovered football when he got to high school. My dad had a saying: "Never quit school. It's the lightest luggage you're ever going to take, and no one can take your education away from you." That's as true now as it ever was, but of my dad's four kids, Rob was the only good student—not including the day he walked home from kindergarten, of course. He and I both went to Scarlett Heights Collegiate, and it was a great school. Part of that was how close-knit our community was; everyone had a couple of brothers or sisters who all went to the same school a few years apart. For the most part, everyone got along with everyone at Scarlett Heights. I don't remember any serious problems with bullying, like you hear about today. I think we all kind of looked after each other. I'd played football since Grade 9. I was a running back in my junior year, then played offensive line as a senior. There were 20 or so high schools in Etobicoke back then—enough to form a good-sized league with a south division and a north division. The finals would be at Centennial Park in late autumn. Our big rival was Richview Collegiate. Even outside of school, we weren't friendly with the Richview kids. We would stick to our neighbourhood, and they would stick to theirs. (Ironically, my four daughters and my nephew Michael all ended up going to Richview and had a great time there.)

In any case, I was in Grade 13 and playing on the senior team by the time Rob started Grade 9. Rob played centre. My team, overall, was better than his—I mean we had a bigger number of more talented athletes than his team did. His team did win the juniors once, but they just didn't have the depth my age group had. That being said, Rob personally took football a lot more seriously than I ever did. He attended some training camps in the US, and he used to jog like crazy. Mile after mile. He knew he had a tendency to be heavy, and he was self-conscious about that, so he got out and hit the track as much as he could. Believe it or not, when Rob was in high school, he was a pretty slim guy.

Other than helping out with the family business, Rob got his first job during the summer after he'd finished Grade 10. One of our teachers at Scarlett Heights was married to a man who had a road repair contracting outfit. They needed a lot of workers, especially in the summer, and high school guys were pretty much the perfect fit for something like that (the same way some of my peers and I got jobs at Canada Packers), so Rob and a few of his friends were hired. Their work was tarring the cracks in the roads. I don't remember what Rob was getting paid, but I knew it was good money for a guy his age—which was more than fair, because the work was hard and went right through the heat of the summer. From Grade 10 until he finished high school, Rob worked on that crew in the summertime; years later, as a councillor and then as mayor, he made pothole repair one of his main issues, and I'm sure that old job of his was the inspiration.

After he graduated from Grade 13, he went to Carleton University in Ottawa. My dad and I drove him up there at the beginning of the year; he was living in a rundown house just off campus with a few other guys. The degree Rob was going to take was in business administration, but his main focus was football. Carleton had a team called the Ravens. They were pretty good; they'd won the Dunsmore Cup in 1985 and usually made it into the semi-finals each year. Rob tried out and made the team.

University-level football, unfortunately, turned out to be a bit of a disappointment for him. I remember talking to him on the phone while he was up there in Ottawa. He mainly stayed on the bench with the first-year guys. They only ever got to play once in a blue moon for special teams.

Rob also missed Toronto. I completely understand that—I've never liked being away for long either. After some time at Carleton, he transferred to York University and did another year there. He didn't play football at York, but now that he was back home, he started coaching at the high school level, right back at Scarlett Heights, where it had all begun. Right away, he took to coaching the same way he'd played: he was intense, demanding and very competitive. Rob was shy most of the time—he always had been—but he found his element whenever he got out onto the football field or hockey rink. *That* Rob was a beast.

Anyway, it didn't take long for Rob to realize he just wasn't content with the direction in which his life was going, so he quit York and came to work at Deco. It was pretty similar to the path I'd taken, which is another story, but by this point, it was the early 1990s and my older brother, Randy, and I were both at Deco.

Growing up, Randy was always a "rough and ready" sort, one of the toughest guys in the neighbourhood. He had more than his share of scraps. But Randy always cared a great deal for the people around him. He would give them the shirt off his back if they needed it. His scrapping tendencies calmed down a lot the older he got, as well. These days, he's doing a great job running Deco Toronto.

Rob worked in the back and on the factory floor, and he also worked in our sales department, where I was. It was great to have him there—Deco truly felt like a family business with Rob on board. But he wasn't going to stay more than a few years. Rob had a different calling. He just hadn't figured it out yet.

DIANE FORD

When Rob was really little, I took him everywhere. You could even say I spoiled him a little. My other three kids were already in school, but Rob was my baby. We'd go grocery shopping together all the time, and it wasn't until a few years ago, as an adult, he finally said, "You know, Mom, I hated going grocery shopping." We lived in Etobicoke, and Rob was this cute little blond kid. One day when he was about three years old, he slipped out of the house. I normally checked on him—when he was playing and I was doing housework—every five or ten minutes or so, but somehow he slipped out.

When I finally noticed he was gone, I had a bit of a panic. I went outside, went around the corner, calling his name, and still couldn't find him, so I was almost on the verge of phoning the police. Then, all of a sudden, our Italian neighbour a few doors down opened her door and said, "Oh, Mrs. Ford, Rob's over here. He's having some spaghetti." I was still feeling a bit panicky, so I asked her why she'd let him in and fed him instead of bringing him back home. She only shrugged, smiled and said, "He's been here to eat a few times before, Mrs. Ford." I'd had no idea about that, but back then, that was the kind of neighbourhood we lived in, safe and trustworthy.

As kids, Doug and Rob were both very easy to raise. Doug always looked out for Rob because there were five years between them. Everybody seems to think they're closer in age, but there are five years. When they got older, I guess they got into scraps amongst themselves, because they were brothers. But none of these scraps was ever really major. I remember one story in particular where their personalities showed through. Doug was in high school at the time, so Rob was still in public school. Anyway, their rooms were both a complete mess. So I let loose on them. I said, "Look, you guys. I want your rooms cleaned up. I'm going out shopping, and if they're not done by the time I get home, you're going to be in trouble, and I mean it. I mean it. You'll be grounded." I really laid the law down with the two of them.

After I was finished speaking, Doug came up and gave me a big hug. "Oh, Mom," he said, "I'm sorry. I know, I know. I really should have done it already." That was Doug. Always a schmoozer, even as a kid. He could talk his way out of almost anything.

But then there was Rob, who said, "You're always on my back about something, Mom!" That was the difference between the two of them. Rob wasn't a schmoozer at all. He always had his own mind. He would get downright stubborn if he really, really believed in something. Once he believed in something, you'd have to prove it was otherwise for him to change his mind. He had the strength of his convictions, his whole life long.

Rob was very good at public speaking, but offstage, he was always very shy. When he was a kid and he'd have to do a speech for school, I would coach him. The kids in his class would have to pick something they wanted to talk about and then get up and deliver it. Since Rob loved hockey so much, he chose Bobby Orr. As it turned out, I had just finished taking a public speaking course. Since Doug Sr and I were both heavily involved with Rotary, I had to give a lot of speeches at various events, but I'd been nervous about it, same as Rob, so I took a course. Anyway, there were a lot of things I picked up from that public speaking course that I passed on to Rob. I told him, "Instead of just saying when Bobby Orr was born and such and such, what you have to do, Rob, is get your audience's attention, so what's a good opening? What does Bobby Orr do the best?"

"He scores," said Rob.

"Okay," I said. "You've got your opener."

We developed the speech from there, and when Rob presented it to his class, he just stood up and shouted, "He shoots, he scores!" That got all his classmates' attention. He did very well with that speech, which in turn gave him a sense of confidence he hadn't had before. His shyness never went away, but at least he knew how to speak well in public. I was glad to have played a small part in that.

I saw Rob's strong convictions again when he became a teenager. As he was finishing public school, he started putting on weight. He was 13, going into high school, and he was embarrassed that other kids would make fun of him for being fat. So that summer, after he'd finished Grade 8, he came home every day and made himself a tuna sandwich. He was running all the time, too, but his diet he especially took hold of and did all by himself. There was his determination again, because once he got going, he didn't quit. Rob lost 50 pounds in two months. He looked like a different kid altogether when he started high school.

A year later, Rob was really in shape, because he'd made it onto his school's football team, and his dad sent him down to a football training camp at Notre Dame for the summer. That was Rob's "vacation"—but it was really anything but. The people running the training camp were very strict. They made Rob and all those other young guys run around and around all the time. Rob later said he didn't have a minute to himself that whole summer. He said that sometimes their running route took them past the big golden arches of a McDonald's near the camp, but if they went to McDonald's, they weren't allowed to practise football the next day. That whole summer, he told me, he couldn't stop dreaming about having a Big Mac.

CHAPTER 3

Doug and Diane

Rob always loved to help people and give back to his community; it might seem obvious that politics were in his future, but I don't think any of that would have happened without the path set by our dad. So to understand the beginnings of Rob's political career, I think it's important to talk a bit about my dad's story.

Douglas Bruce Ford was born in 1933 and grew up in the east end of Toronto. He was the youngest of nine siblings, and when he was three months old, his father, Ernest, passed away. After my granddad's passing, my grandmother, Celia, was left in a very hard financial situation. She often couldn't manage to pay the rent, so she, my dad and all his brothers and sisters would often have to pack up in the middle of the night and move to somewhere new. They lived in many different apartments, mostly above grocery and variety stores along Jones Avenue and the Danforth.

Because of the poverty of his childhood, my dad dropped out of school after Grade 9 and went to work as soon as he could. It was under these circumstances, I believe, that he developed his tireless work ethic, and by the time he was 16, he had two jobs on the go: one as a lifeguard at the swimming pool at Glenview Terrace (Dad was a marathon swimmer in his youth, but as part of his training regimen, he was expected to lifeguard at the pool), and one doing odd jobs through the General Steel Wares downtown. He managed to save up enough to move out on his own and buy a Triumph motorcycle. In the early 1950s, while lifeguarding at the pool, he met a woman named Diane Campbell.

They got to know each other at the pool, and as the family story goes, one day he offered to give her a ride home. She lived up at Bathurst and Lawrence and was happy to accept a ride rather than take the TTC all the way home. Walking out to the parking lot, she spotted a Lincoln and a Cadillac, and she started to get excited . . . until she saw the motorbike parked *between* the Lincoln and the Caddy.

"Hop on!" said my dad.

My mother-to-be was doubtful. She'd always been warned never to get on a bike. Back in those days, the city used to oil the roads to keep the dust down, especially in the warmer, drier months of the year. She could imagine how easily the bike could slide out of control on an oiled road. But at the same time, it was a long, uncomfortable trip home on the TTC, and besides, she kind of liked the hard-working young man who was offering her the ride. So next thing she knew, she was climbing onto the bike behind him.

Dad kicked the bike into gear and set off. Sure enough, though, he hit an oil patch and they wiped out. Luckily, he hadn't been going too fast and neither of them were hurt—but, according to the story, he jumped up and ran right past my mother, apparently to make sure his bike was okay before checking on his passenger or himself! I personally don't know how true this story is. These kinds of stories tend to get embellished over time, but it has definitely become an infamous bit of Ford family history.

Anyway, despite the crash and the story that goes with it, my mom started to take a real shine to my dad, and before much longer, they became a couple, even though they were both still teenagers. My mother's family wasn't nearly as poor as my dad's, but they weren't rich either, and my maternal grandfather, Clarence Campbell, was hesitant about his daughter's boyfriend, who came from a rough neighbourhood and had dropped out of school. But Clarence couldn't deny how hard a worker my dad was, either, and eventually accepted the fact that he'd become part of Diane's life.

My mom and dad were married in September 1956. Dad went on to a couple of new jobs: he drove a police tow truck for a while, and he also worked in sales for Swift, a meat-packing company in Toronto's Stockyards neighbourhood. I mention Swift especially because, as a teenager, I also went to work in the meat-packing industry, although what I was doing was not sales. In any case, in 1956, Ted Herriott, a neighbour, helped my dad get a job at a company called Avery Label, where he worked. Avery had recently opened up in Canada and was looking for another salesman. My dad applied. Avery offered him $55 a week, plus commission. When he compared this to the $35 a week he was making at his other jobs, it was a pretty easy decision, and so began his career in label printing.

Dad stayed on at Avery for the next six years and was a key part of the organization as it started its Canadian subsidiary. He made his mark cold-calling and selling to companies like Swift and Canada Packers; places or industries where he'd worked and understood the needs. Within a few years he became Avery Canada's top salesman. It seemed he'd found his calling—and it didn't take him long to decide he wanted to do it for himself.

So one day in 1962, not long after my older brother, Randy, was born, my dad came home and told my mom that he'd quit Avery. He and Ted Herriott were going to start their own company, Dad told her. I don't know how she took the news, but I do know that Dad used to say he was lucky if he had $10 in the bank in those days, so it must have been nerve-racking for her. Still, she knew what a go-getter and hard worker he was, and if anyone could pull it off, it was him.

Dad and Ted named their business Deco. Their first office space was on Bathurst Street. It wasn't much, just a small room with a shared desk and a telephone. Their method at the beginning was purely outsourcing to another label company and making a small percentage from the sale. It was a good start, but it wasn't going to make them a lot of money. In fact, Dad realized early on that he'd need to cut out the supplier altogether, and to do that, he would need his own label presses, as well as a bigger space. So in a couple of years, he bought Ted out for $30,000 and struck off on his own.

The next thing Dad did was travel to Japan, since the Japanese were manufacturing some of the best label presses in the industry at a reasonable cost. He ended up buying three presses for $10,000, but he was also amazed by the Japanese work ethic and sense of honour. He said he'd purchased the presses on a handshake alone, only saying what he wanted and when he needed them delivered. Sure enough, three presses showed up in Canada—with extra parts—on the agreed-upon date. (It wasn't just Japan that impressed my dad; he was so amazed by the Asian culture and work ethic in general that he took Rob and me there many years later, on one of the most unforgettable trips of our lives.) With his three presses, Dad then rented a bigger industrial space on Martin Grove Road, where he stayed for the next five or six years as Deco grew.

The first few years were especially hard, which is usually the case for any successful entrepreneur. Dad worked at it seven days a week. Mom helped out with the books and the accounting, in addition to being a stay-at-home mother to four kids. Even we kids helped out, putting together little sample bags on our basement Ping-Pong table. Dad would distribute the sample bags to potential customers as part of his sales pitch. He paid us for our efforts, too—half a cent per bag. Looking back, I think of that as a pretty vital lesson he was teaching us: nothing would come for free, there would not be a silver spoon, but if we did put in the work, we would earn some money.

Despite how tough he was, and how hard he was working, Dad came home for supper every night. Our family meant everything to him, and I have many fond memories of him taking us fishing up near Burleigh Falls, northwest of Belleville. He was also passionate about giving back to his community. For instance, he and my mother were both lifelong Rotarians, and Dad was made a Paul Harris Fellow for the endless work he did on behalf of the organization over the years. (I'm proud to say my mother and I both went on to receive the same honour.) We even said the Rotary Grace before every dinner: "Lord, we stand from every race, from every creed, from every place. We give our thanks." In addition to Rotary, Dad sat on the board of governors of Etobicoke General Hospital for many years and was instrumental in helping raise $2 million for the first CT scanner the hospital was able to obtain.

Dad's dedication to his community came from how poor he was growing up. He'd had nothing. Absolutely nothing. And though he worked hard, he also believed he was very fortunate to achieve what he'd achieved, and so he wanted to give back. Giving back to your community is one of the values he absolutely instilled in us. It doesn't matter if it's coaching your kid's soccer team, donating your time and money to a group like Rotary, or volunteering with your local hospital—you have to give back. That was a lesson Rob and I both took to heart as we grew into adults.

Deco had started to turn a good profit by 1970, a year or so after Rob was born. Not long after that, Dad had a house custom-built for our family: a big ranch-style six-bedroom at 15 Weston Wood Road, off Royal York. We moved there when I was eight years old and Rob was three. That house would be the site of many Ford-hosted parties over the years to come. (No backyard in Canada has hosted more people in the last two decades—close to 200,000.) My mother, Diane, still lives in that house. I visit on a regular basis, and so did Rob until his passing. It's funny how a family home has a way of defining you.

Deco's growing success also allowed Dad to buy the industrial space on Greensboro Drive, where we've been to this day. He paid $400,000 in the late 1970s for 10,000 square feet (we've since expanded the building to 50,000 square feet and have manufacturing facilities in Chicago and New Jersey). That allowed him to bring in more equipment and more employees, which in turn made it possible for him to take on a lot more business. Life went on from there, and Deco only got more successful. It eventually became my career as well, but that's something I'll talk about later.

CHAPTER 4

Deco

In the fall of 1987, we took a trip to Asia for two weeks—my dad, Rob and I. I was 23 at the time and Rob was 18. On one level, it was a business trip, but it was also a learning experience. Looking back, I think the learning aspect of the trip was more important to my dad. He'd always had a lot of respect for the Asian work ethic and business practices, and I think he wanted to expose us to that. We flew from Toronto to LA, and from LA to Tokyo. In Tokyo, there was a layover, and then we flew to Seoul, South Korea. We spent three days there, meeting with various business connections and seeing how their labelling industry worked. There was very little space in this Korean factory. The workers were operating in a tiny industrial unit. Their label press was down in a pit, similar to the pits in garages where you get your oil changed. And the workers were operating with this amazing efficiency, moving up and down from the pit, using the press.

"See?" said my dad. "See what they're doing? Talk about utilizing your space!"

From Seoul we went to Taipei. It was late at night when we landed, and then we hopped straight onto a bus. As the bus took us down the highway through the centre of Taipei, I remember seeing what looked like millions of mopeds. Mopeds everywhere. I'd never seen so many mopeds in my life. We got off at our hotel, a place called Asiaworld, and here was something straight out of the movies: outside the hotel's main entrance was a guy with his jacket open, showing us all these knock-off watches. Then we went inside the hotel. The interior was massive. It was circular and open, all the way to the top, and on each floor around the circle, you could see the rooms. The funniest part was that the place seemed absolutely empty. It felt like we were the only guests there. The people at the front desk gave us the key to our room. We went up and opened the door, and when I closed it behind us, the handle came off in my hand. Rob and I had to wedge a chair up against the door to keep it shut.

On the other side of the room was a huge purple window, dome-shaped, like a skylight. Dad went to the window and looked out. Out past the lights of the city was a mountain range, although it was hard to make out against the night sky.

"We're going way up there into the mountains tomorrow," said Dad.

I wasn't happy to hear that, and I don't think Rob was either. We were both more than a little homesick. But we were here to learn, and we knew how much Dad admired the Asian way of doing business. So first thing in the morning, we left the hotel and hopped on another bus. I couldn't read any of the signs because everything was written in Mandarin.

Over the next couple of hours, the bus chugged up into the mountains on the outskirts of the city, and by midday we'd arrived in a little industrial village. The three of us got off the bus, and right away, Dad went to find his contact, leaving us in the central square. So there we were, Rob and I, two homesick white guys with our blond hair. The people in the village seemed very nice but also openly curious. They all kind of circled around us, checking us out, talking and laughing with each other. Rob and I ended up standing back to back. We were naive enough to be nervous. Just then, our dad came back, and he thought it was hilarious. He knew everything was all right, and he thought it was funny to see his two younger sons out of their element like that.

Anyway, Dad had come back to us with his contact, a Taiwanese man who specialized in North American relations for a local factory that made label presses. He spoke

English, and he led us through the village to go see the factory. The factory was composed of some Quonset huts, where the various components were made. It was siesta time for the workers, and they were all sleeping on collapsed cardboard boxes on the ground. We had to step over them to make our way around. I think that's what I remember best about Taichung: all those workers taking a nap right on the spot. When they woke up, they'd be right back to work. That was a work ethic I'd never seen before, and it was exactly what Dad had intended for us to see.

After Taiwan, the third leg of our Asia trip was Hong Kong, which was still a British colony at that time. The city was booming. I felt like I could see money and prosperity everywhere. I remember going up a back alley with Rob, then taking a little freight elevator to a room above street level, and in this room were all these wooden carvings. An old man was sitting there chiselling them all by hand. I think I bought six of them on the spot, at $20 apiece. It was a lot of money then, but today you would pay a fortune for something handmade like that. I think what impressed us most was watching this man work, chiselling away, completely dedicated to what he was doing.

Hong Kong was the last stop of the trip, and from there we flew home, again via LA. Rob and I joked that we would kiss the ground in Toronto once we arrived. The trip had been a long haul, and we'd been culture-shocked, but

Dad had intended it to be a learning experience and that's exactly what it was. He had huge admiration for Asia, ever since his trip to Japan. Up to the day he died, he used to ship all these artifacts and sculptures and art home, and he'd display them in our family's house. Here in Toronto, Dad spent a lot of time in Chinatown, taking in the culture and learning how things were done.

Rob was as glad to get home from that trip as I was, but I know it had a huge effect on him too. Up until the day he died, whenever he saw signs for things like Oriental furniture or Oriental rugs, he would remember that trip and talk about what we saw. (Many years after the trip, in fact, when Rob was a city councillor, he made a remark about how "those Oriental people work like dogs; they sleep beside their machines." Some people found this comment offensive, but Rob meant it with utmost respect toward the Asian community, and as a recollection of what we saw on our trip. He also got tons of emails and phone calls from Asian Canadians thanking him for the remark. It might not have been "politically correct," but it came from a place of respect.)

CHAPTER 5

Entering the Fray

In 1994, I met a man named Doug Holyday. He was an Etobicoke city councillor who wanted to run for mayor (this was before the megacity amalgamation, when Etobicoke was still its own municipality). Doug came into Deco to have some campaign labels printed up. Along with him was another councillor, Brian Flynn, who was the son of former Etobicoke mayor Dennis Flynn. Doug Holyday intended to campaign against Bruce Sinclair, who'd been mayor since 1984.

My first meeting with Doug was strictly business—it was about the printing of his campaign materials. I had no personal interest in politics at that time. But I took a liking to Doug almost right away. He was a conservative, for starters, and there were a lot of changes he wanted to make, especially with privatizing certain services and taking on the status quo. He also struck me as just a good guy, down to earth, honest and principled. He didn't come across as a sleazy politician. After we got to know each other a little better, he asked me if I'd be willing to come out and help him knock on doors and put up signs.

Again, I wasn't involved in politics before that, but since Doug only had a small campaign team and nobody expected he could beat Sinclair, I agreed to lend a hand. So before long, I found myself knocking on doors up Kipling, Islington and Royal York Road. I did it every night after work. When people answered their doors, I would say, "I'm campaigning on behalf of Doug Holyday. He's running for mayor, and we'd appreciate your support. May I put up a sign on your property?" Simple as that. It didn't take long for me to really enjoy it—it was a little like cold-call sales—and I ended up putting up hundreds of signs for Doug's campaign. I loved the feeling of driving along Islington and seeing all those signs and knowing that was my work.

As things turned out, Doug did beat Sinclair that year, and he became the final mayor of Etobicoke, before the amalgamation in 1998. Doug was a great mayor, too. He saved Etobicoke over a million dollars a year by privatizing garbage collection and buying out city employees' accumulated sick-leave plans. He remains a good friend to this day, and I like to blame him for getting the Fords into politics.

That's not to say my dad or Rob were interested in the beginning, when I was helping Doug campaign. They didn't get involved with it at all. But after Doug beat Sinclair, I thought, "Boy, this is a lot easier than I expected. We can get someone elected!"

It just so happened that Doug's campaign and election came at a time when Dad was finally slowing down at Deco and spending a lot more time at home—or "getting in my hair," as my mom would say. The other thing going on was the fourth year of the provincial New Democratic Party government under Premier Bob Rae.

The Rae government had been voted in in 1990, and although they'd been popular for their first six months, they plummeted in the polls after that. For one thing, the province was in the middle of a brutal recession, the worst downturn since the Great Depression. As a result, the Rae government had had to backtrack on most of their campaign promises. Like many other Ontarians, especially conservatives like him, my dad couldn't stand the NDP government and their management of the province. He would yell at the TV whenever Bob Rae came on.

Dad wasn't accomplishing anything with all the yelling—other than driving my mother crazy. But there was a provincial general election coming up, so I paid a visit to the Ontario Progressive Conservative Riding Association for Etobicoke-Humber and registered my dad as a candidate. Then I went home and told him I'd put his name in.

He was not impressed. "I'm not going to be a damn politician," he said. "I can't stand politicians."

I knew what strategy I needed to use to convince him. Dad had an almost overwhelming sense of civic duty and believed in helping the needy. He knew how hard poverty is. As a child, he'd woken up many mornings with no food in the cupboard. He would say to Rob and me, "You guys have no idea what it's like to have nothing." When it came to social issues, my dad always defended the less fortunate. With his business success, he'd become almost obsessed with helping people and giving back—so much so that Rob and I started calling him "Dipper" (a play on the term "NDPer") as a joke. It really *was* a joke; Dad couldn't stand the NDP and had been a card-carrying member of the Progressive Conservatives all his adult life. He believed—as I do—that the Tories were the only party with the business sense and financial policies to make things work efficiently, which in turn is best for everyone.

His sense of civic duty was what Rob and I appealed to, as well as the fact that all his yelling at the TV wasn't fixing anything. Bit by bit, we wore him down, and finally he agreed. That was good, because his name was already in the hat.

The nomination rally was held at Scarlett Heights, Rob's and my old high school. Our main competition for the nomination was a lawyer named Tom Barlow, who would later go on to represent Rob. (To this day, I'm still friends with Tom, and I think he's one of the classiest guys out there.) It took three or four hours and went to a third ballot before Dad secured the nomination. Then we had to focus on our campaign. The incumbent we were running against was a member of the Liberal Party named Jim Henderson. He'd held Etobicoke-Humber since 1985, even keeping his seat through the NDP wins in 1990. Everybody predicted that Henderson would easily win, but we planned to give him a run for his money. And even though we'd helped out on Doug Holyday's campaign, this was the first full effort for the Ford family.

It was the early spring of 1995. We were in the pre-writ period, where candidates are permitted to get their literature, signs, stickers and handouts ready and prepare their campaign teams for the battle to come. Rob and I called in everybody to help out—our mother, our brother, our sister, members of our extended family, and all the friends we could count on. Our plan was to cover the area as heavily as we could. Jim Henderson may have been the incumbent, but folks in Etobicoke knew us.

We also hired an experienced campaign manager, Ron Thompson, the same person who'd managed Doug Holyday's campaign. His plan was to simplify our approach as much as possible and stick to the PC Party messaging. Fortunately, PC leader Mike Harris had a very straightforward platform: the Common Sense Revolution. The main points of the Common Sense Revolution were balancing the budget, reducing taxes, reducing the overall size of the government, and cutting back on handouts. Mike

Harris himself kept reiterating those messages, and so did we. This couldn't have come at a better time—the people of Ontario were ready for some serious reform after Bob Rae.

A typical campaign day for us started first thing in the morning, as early as six o'clock, when we'd go to the subway stations, and usually lasted until midnight. During Dad's campaign, I made a habit of checking on the other campaign offices in our riding; most of those other teams would be closed by seven or eight o'clock in the evenings. Our office was in a three-storey building in a little pocket of land at Dundas and Kipling (it's not there anymore). We used the same office Doug Holyday had used. Our team were all volunteers, except for the campaign manager, Ron Thompson, whom we paid about $1,000 a week. He was underpaid—all campaign managers are—working 100 hours a week and getting paid as little as possible, because of how tightly a campaign has to adhere to its budget.

Speaking of our budget, in 1995, our campaign budget was no more than $60,000, which we accrued through donations. Our donations consisted of $50 here, $100 there, mainly from people throughout the neighbourhood. In any case, the $60,000 went pretty quickly. That's why campaigning then, same as now, relies so heavily on volunteers. (Luckily, campaigning is fun for the people who care about it, and the contacts you make, no matter what party you're with, often carry on as relationships for years.) In this respect, Rob was instrumental: he got all his high school buddies to help us secure the nomination and then help us on the campaign.

With our office, tight budget, campaign manager and volunteers in hand, we needed to get out there and knock on doors and put up signs, so that's what we did. All of us, even Dad, worked one end of that riding to the other. As I said before, the area had been a very close-knit community for years, so the doors we were knocking on were the homes of people we'd gone to school with, or folks who knew my parents through Rotary, or kids Rob coached. We had a lot of personal connections in Etobicoke-Humber, and that was our true strength. Even people who'd been lifelong Liberals agreed to support my dad, whom they knew, over their traditional party alignment.

Although my dad had been reluctant to get involved at first, it didn't take long before he was as fiercely into the campaign as Rob and I were. It was partly because we'd made it a family initiative. We were all for one and one for all, and once things got going, there was no stopping our collective energy.

Election night was June 8, 1995. We'd gathered the team at the campaign office, and we had scrutineers spread throughout all the different polling stations. There were about 120 polling stations altogether. The polls closed at 9:00 p.m. Then each of our scrutineers would call in as the votes at their polling stations were tallied. We, in turn, would record the totals on a chart on our wall at the campaign office. It didn't take more than 15 or 20 minutes for us to see the pattern emerging. Dad was winning—by a landslide.

Outside our office, outside Etobicoke-Humber, the same thing was happening province-wide. Ridings that had been NDP orange were turning PC blue at a staggering rate. By the time the count was finished, the Tories had won a majority with 82 seats (up from the 20 seats with which they'd started the election). The Liberals had dropped from 36 to 30, and the NDP had dropped from 74 to 17. It was a huge defeat for them, and it wasn't long before Bob Rae resigned.

Jim Henderson, the Liberal incumbent, visited our office that night to congratulate Dad on his win. He was a doctor by profession, and despite our political differences, he struck me as a real gentleman—especially in the way he'd come to admit defeat face-to-face. After he left, we had a celebration at the office. Our team all came together to join in the feeling of our shared victory. Not that we could ride on the feeling of victory for too long; Dad was already biting at the bit to head down to Queen's Park. The Common Sense Revolution had just begun, and there was a lot of work to do.

CHAPTER 6

Dad Leads the Way

They called it the "Class of '95": the PC caucus under Mike Harris that had taken Queen's Park by storm during that provincial election. A lot of the members were political rookies, like my dad. John Baird, Tony Clement and Jim Flaherty—all first-time members—are probably the best-known names from the Class of '95, apart from Harris himself. It was the best political team I've ever seen compiled, and it brought some much-needed repairs to all levels of Canadian politics.

Harris was sworn in as Ontario's 22nd premier in September of that year. Right away, Harris started to cut back on NDP-driven hiring quotas, provincial welfare rates and overstaffed government ministries. He also gave the province's education system a major fix. Ontarians from all walks of life were grateful for these changes, but more than anything, I think they were happy to have a guy leading the province who wasn't just one more politician. Harris was also the kind of person who meant what he said and said what he meant, a real no-bullshit straight shooter, much like my dad. Rob and I both followed his example in our political careers.

When the House first sat that fall, the backbenchers were arranged alphabetically. So my dad, Doug Ford, found himself seated next to Jim Flaherty. The two of them hit it off immediately. Dad said Jim struck him as the kind of guy who could go into the middle of a union hall and drink beers with all the blue-collar workers and have the best time of his life, and he could turn around and go toe to toe with the top financial analysts in the world. "Watch," Dad told me and Rob, "Jim Flaherty is going places."

The Class of '95 worked their asses off. Harris needed all his members, ministers and backbenchers alike, to really put their shoulders to the wheel, since they had a massive agenda to put through in order to make the Common Sense Revolution a reality. In a four-year term, any government usually has only the first two years to make their agenda happen and to keep their promises and commitments. After that two-year mark, it's back to planning and preparing for the next election. Dad's typical day would start at Queen's Park. If the House was sitting, they'd go into the chamber for a question-and-answer period. Most of the time, this would go until noon, but sometimes they'd have to go until eight or nine in the evening, even later once in a while, to make sure the party had enough members to pass a bill when it was voted on.

Otherwise, Dad's main focus was his community, Etobicoke-Humber, and he spent as much time at his constituency office as he could. His constituency office was located at Royal York and Chapman Roads. He would help his constituents with health cards, health issues, transportation concerns and pretty much anything else they brought into his office. A lot of the time, members of the public don't know whose responsibility it is for federal services, provincial services or municipal services. Even politicians get confused about these differences sometimes. It's all too easy not to care or be helpful, but Dad always made a point of getting hold of the appropriate people at the other levels of government when he couldn't directly help to resolve someone's issue.

Though my dad wasn't a cabinet minister, he had a presence that was noted by a lot of his fellow MPPs, no matter their party. This was something Jim Flaherty talked about when he gave the eulogy at my dad's funeral in 2006. For instance, my dad was part of a committee that would regularly visit Northern Ontario. The committee was made up of NDP, Liberal and PC members. They would fly to Timmins on a Bearskin Airlines flight. As Jim said in the eulogy, my dad wasn't the cabinet minister, but he was the unofficial leader of the group. As soon as they'd land, Dad would take charge and say, "First we go to the liquor store, then we get some sandwiches, then we go back to the hotel and get down to business." It was this kind of approach that held him in good standing all across the House.

Dad had a good relationship with Mike Harris as well. For starters, he respected Harris and truly believed in the Common Sense Revolution. Dad was also a team player and helped out wherever he could. But most importantly, he wasn't afraid to speak up. At caucus meetings, many of the MPPs, especially the backbenchers, were afraid to speak up in front of Mike Harris. The late Al Palladini, who was the minister of transportation in the Class of '95, said to me once, "Man, your dad has balls." Al went on to tell me how my dad just got up in the middle of one of these big caucus meetings and held Mike Harris to account for not returning a phone call from one of the voters in Etobicoke-Humber. Harris told my dad he got thousands of calls. And my dad, according to Palladini, said, "I don't care, just make sure you return this guy's call." The whole caucus meeting went silent and everything became very tense. Finally, Harris just broke up laughing and said, "I'll call the guy back, Doug, don't worry."

To Dad, constituents were customers, so he brought the same approach to politics as he did to business—

customer service excellence. Everyone gets called back. It was his golden rule. At Deco, we still live by that. As far as Dad's constituency work went, Rob and I were helping him out. Like I said, if someone called, we would make sure the call was returned. In some cases, we would go to their house to help them out. I found that knocking on one person's door usually led to a visit not just with them but with their neighbours as well. Maybe the people across the street would come out and ask to have a problem solved. Rob and I both loved going door to door and meeting people on Dad's behalf. That, I think, is when we really knew that politics was in our blood—Rob's especially.

I always said that if Rob could have met everyone in Toronto one-on-one, they would have had an entirely different opinion of him.

CHAPTER 7

Lessons from Our Father

Mike Harris's government was at the end of their first term in 1999, and they had lots to be proud of before going up for re-election. A huge number of new jobs had been created in Ontario, unemployment had been reduced, and provincial tax revenues had been boosted. More than anything, Mike Harris had proved to be a man who kept his promises. One of the biggest legacies of the PC's first term was a large number of mergers at the municipal level throughout the province.

The biggest of these mergers, of course, was the creation of the Toronto "megacity," which amalgamated the separate cities of Toronto, East York, North York, York, Scarborough and Etobicoke into one. This occurred in 1998. Our friend Doug Holyday, who'd been serving as the mayor of Etobicoke, ran for and was elected as a councillor in the megacity government. The first mayor of the new Toronto was Mel Lastman.

A similar redistribution occurred at the provincial level as well, where the map of Ontario's ridings was redrawn to align with the federal ridings. This meant 27 fewer seats—and 27 fewer MPPs—in the legislature. One of the new ridings was Etobicoke Centre, which was a merger of Etobicoke West and Etobicoke-Humber, my dad's riding. The MPP of Etobicoke West was a man named Chris Stockwell. Also a Tory, Chris had been elected as Speaker of the Ontario legislature in 1996. He was very popular in his home riding. We knew his family, including his father, Bill (who'd been a municipal politician many years before), very well.

Chris and my dad both decided to run for Etobicoke Centre, but it meant starting the nomination process all over again. The nomination was heated right from the get-go. Between Chris's supporters and ours, we had over 3,000 people. The only place we could fit them all was at the Centennial Park auditorium. The truth is, in spite of the amazing support from all the people who knew us, and in spite of how hard Rob and I were pushing him, my dad's heart wasn't in it anymore. He was 65 by then and he was tired. Chris, on the other hand, was only in his early 40s. By the end of the nomination day, Chris Stockwell had won the PC ticket for Etobicoke Centre. When the election was held in June of that year, 1999, Chris won the riding, beating the Liberal candidate by 6,000 votes. Mike Harris appointed Chris minister of labour, and he succeeded Jim Flaherty in the role. Jim had gone on to fill the position of attorney-general of Ontario.

MORE THAN ANYTHING, Dad was relieved when his political career came to an end in 1999. He set his sights on proper retirement, which meant spending time down in Florida with my mom. Sadly, though, he didn't get to enjoy his retirement for very long. In 2006, Dad was diagnosed with colon cancer. In a very short time, the sickness completely devastated him. I remember how, close to the end, he kept asking Rob and me about when we were going to have that year's Ford Fest, our annual barbecue for family and friends. Dad seemed really intent on enjoying one last big party with everyone.

We had Ford Fest on September 20 of that year. Mike Harris, who'd been retired from politics since 2002, and Jim Flaherty, who by then was serving as federal minister of finance under Stephen Harper, both came over to visit. Rob and I helped Dad down from his room and brought him into the living room. He and Jim and Mike sat together and chatted for quite a while, laughing about their time together in the provincial legislature. Finally,

Jim and Mike helped my dad back upstairs to his room to rest. They never saw him again; Dad passed away two days later at Etobicoke General.

Jim Flaherty gave the eulogy at Dad's funeral, and we buried him at Riverside Cemetery. In 2010, Weston Wood Park was renamed Douglas B. Ford Park in Dad's honour. You can see the park from our family home.

There were two main lessons we took away from Dad's political legacy. The first was his commitment to customer service excellence. The golden rule about always calling people back was only one part of that commitment. The bigger picture was the responsibility to take care of our constituents all the time. Nothing was more important, according to Dad, than the people of Etobicoke. He'd learned not to get caught up in all the garbage downtown at Queen's Park, and instead, kept his focus on his riding. If his constituents were having a fight with the government, then the constituents were always right, because there are few things more infuriating than trying to fight through government bureaucracy. The second lesson was that in politics, you can only really trust the person you see in the mirror every morning. Many other people in politics will smile at you as quickly as they'll take a knife and stab you in the back. He taught us that politics is a game where most of the players are trying to get ahead by any means necessary, no matter how dirty the tricks are that they have to use. Honest, straight shooters are few and far between, but when they do appear—guys like Mike Harris and Jim Flaherty, for example—they can really get things done, because the people know they can trust them. Dad, in turn, was a straight shooter with Mike Harris, and Harris respected him for it.

I remember how Rob was fascinated with Dad's political career. Rob was working at Deco when Dad was serving as an MPP, but Rob didn't take to the family business the way I did. And whereas Rob and I were both passionate about helping Dad—for example, by getting out there and pounding the pavement on his behalf—I know that Rob had finally figured out his own true calling.

CHAPTER 8

A Man of the People

I hear it from tourists and other politicians . . . People make fun of us. A lot of people compare [Toronto city council] politics to the Leafs: a bunch of misfits who couldn't organize a two-car funeral. Politicians in other cities tell me, "You guys are as dysfunctional as the Blue Jays."[1]

—Rob Ford, in an interview with the *Toronto Sun*, 2009

As I look back, I think Rob definitely had a long-term plan from the very beginning. He wouldn't have stopped at being the mayor of Toronto. I know that if he was healthy and alive today, he could run for the leadership of the PC Party in Ontario, and I'm sure he would be chosen. From provincial politics, he might've even gone into the federal arena. He really liked Ottawa from his time at Carleton, and going back there to pursue his passion was not at all out of the question.

But when he was just starting out, he chose municipal politics. This was because the municipal level is more hand-to-hand with the constituents. From my own time as a councillor, I've learned there's no level of politics more engaging than municipal, because it affects the day-to-day life of every individual. This kind of service was what appealed to Rob, especially with our dad already working at the provincial level.

The first time Rob ran for office was in 1997. At that time, Dad and the rest of the Class of '95 had been in their seats for two years—there wouldn't be another provincial general election until 1999. Rob decided to keep it local, so he set his sights—at least for the beginning of his political career (and he was still only in his mid-20s)—on serving at the municipal level. Toronto's first election as an amalgamated megacity was about to get underway. Rob put in for Ward 3 (Kingsway-Humber). At that time, each ward had two councillors. Among the other candidates, Rob would be running against Gloria Lindsay Luby, a former school board trustee who'd been an Etobicoke councillor since 1985.

I got out there with Rob, knocking on doors and putting up signs. This was my third time assisting on a campaign, after the work I'd done on Doug Holyday's and my dad's. Unfortunately, Rob didn't win his first time around. Lindsay Luby took one of the Kingsway-Humber councillor seats with 13,123 votes; a guy named Mario Giansante took the second seat with 12,767 votes. The old mayor of Etobicoke, Dennis Flynn, came in third place with 10,092. Rob, in fourth place, had still managed to pull in well over 9,000 votes—which was the most votes for any first-time candidate in the city. Not bad for a rookie who was pretty unknown in the community back then.

He was not happy, but he was satisfied with his results. I was proud of him. On top of that, it had been a tough race. Rob had done well, and we knew the next election would only be a few years away. In the meantime, he just came back to Deco and kept working in sales. He was a good salesman. He had the same approach to sales as he did to politics: door-to-door customer service. It worked well for him, even if it wasn't his passion.

Outside Etobicoke, the only two serious candidates for mayor were Mel Lastman and Barbara Hall. Hall had served as mayor of Toronto before the amalgamation. Lastman, meanwhile, had been mayor of North York. He was also the founder of Bad Boy Furniture and was a pretty colourful character. He beat Barbara Hall by a fairly slim margin. Lastman's term as mayor was an interesting one. In 1999, he called out the army to deal with a bad snowstorm. He got photographed shaking hands and hanging around with some members of the Hells Angels Motorcycle Club, which the media of course put a scandalous spin on. He managed to piss off the International Olympic Committee—which would arguably cost Toronto its 2008 hosting bid—when he made a public joke about ending up in a cooking pot in Africa. Despite these hiccups, Mayor Mel did quite a few good things for Toronto. His biggest accomplishment, in my opinion, was getting the Sheppard subway line built. Toronto needed subways then as much as it needs them now, and Lastman was a guy who understood that. Rob and our family had a great deal of respect for Mayor Mel.

Anyway, by 2000, Rob was ready to have a go at it again. City council had been reorganized into 44 wards with one councillor each, so the election in 2000 was going to have a lot of incumbents battling it out to keep their seats. This time around, we were more seasoned and had a better idea of how to approach the campaign.

Kingsway-Humber, now renamed Etobicoke Centre, was shaping up to be a fight between Gloria Lindsay Luby and Mario Giansante, since only one of them could stay on as councillor. We looked at the map and came up with a plan. I can't remember if it was Rob's idea or mine, but we decided Rob should run in Etobicoke North. We knew instantly it was the right call. It was a very working-class area and home to a lot of new immigrants. These were the kinds of folks who wanted their politicians to be straight shooters and manage their taxes in a fair way. These were people who didn't have a voice of their own in how municipal decisions were being made. Rob wanted to be their voice, to fight for them, to fix their fences and sidewalks, to do whatever they needed. The incumbent up there was Elizabeth Brown, who'd been a councillor for two terms. She got Mel Lastman's endorsement, but I didn't think she was all that strong as a councillor. The people whose doors we knocked on didn't really know her.

So we got out on the streets in full force, knocking on doors, meeting all the people we could. We had a bigger and better team. Rob was more mature. Part of Etobicoke North had been in our dad's provincial riding. Dad had a good reputation—it all went back to his dedication to the community and customer service—and that worked in Rob's favour, especially as Dad became active in our campaign. We also sent out some literature from Jim Flaherty, who was the attorney-general at the time. In the literature, Jim talked about crime in Etobicoke North, which in turn gave Rob the chance to talk about community resources and crime reduction. We put up as many signs as we could. And this time around, we printed *bigger* signs, almost like mini-billboards. Before long, all you could see on Dixon Road or Rexdale Boulevard was Rob's name.

Election night was in November. We were all together at the campaign office. When the votes were tallied, Elizabeth

Brown had pulled in a little over 4,000. Rob, meanwhile, finished with just under 6,000. He'd won. He was on his way to Toronto city council, and things were never going to be the same.

RENATA FORD

Rob and I first met in high school. We were in different groups of friends, but we knew each other. After high school, I worked at Deco for a year. Later on, when Rob's father was running for the province, Rob came to our door to talk about the campaign. I was single at the time, so my mom gave Rob my phone number. Then we went for coffee and started dating. Four years later, we got married.

The first time Rob ran for city council, he lost. Then the second time around, he tried again and won. I was proud of him because I knew he had a good heart and he was doing the right thing. I come from a Polish family; my parents had to immigrate to Canada for political reasons, so I know about corruption and things like that. I knew those were the kinds of problems Rob wanted to solve. He and I both shared a drive and passion to help people who weren't being taken care of right, so I was happy he became a councillor.

I remember one of the first times Rob went into a council session. He stood up and became very vocal about an issue. Afterwards, Doug Holyday, who was one of Rob's mentors, said, "Oh my goodness, we finally have someone here who has a voice!" Doug joked that Rob was probably waking up all the senior citizens who were watching the council session on TV. But right from the beginning, Rob wanted to change the corruption and the spending and the way other councillors were taking advantage of the system, so he wasn't holding back.

MICHAEL FORD

Rob was a huge part of my life. He was a role model to me and helped me set the path to what I wanted. Rob was involved in my life ever since I can remember. Many times, he was a father figure to me, because my own mother and father had tremendous struggles of their own, so Rob was always very present as I grew up. Especially as I developed an interest in politics, Rob was there. One of my fondest memories is him bringing me down to city hall during a council session. He had me sit in the stands, so I could watch the session go back and forth. This was prior to him being mayor, and I was very young.

In fact, there's a picture of me at six years old, sitting in Rob's campaign office back in 2000. As I ran for city council, I had a running joke with my campaign manager. I would say to him, "Are you coming out door knocking today?" And he would say, "I've been knocking on doors as long as you've been alive." So I would show him that picture of me in Rob's campaign office, back when I was six, and say, "Buddy, I don't think I'm too far behind you."

Anyway, Rob would also bring me down to Nathan Phillips Square every New Year's Eve, for the big bash that Citytv hosted. And outside of politics, there were countless Leafs games and football games he took me to as well. When I was in middle school, I helped him with his football coaching at Don Bosco just about every day. I have many, many good memories of the times I spent with Rob.

CHAPTER 9

Rob's First Years

I attended the inauguration at city hall after Rob was first voted in as a councillor. To some degree, it was the same old, same old, because many long-time politicians were in their same old seats. There were Giorgio Mammoliti, Frances Nunziata, Howard Moscoe, Joe Pantalone, Norm Kelly and our old friend Doug Holyday. There was also a councillor by the name of Jack Layton, whom Rob ended up sitting beside once the city clerk published the council chamber seating plan.

For the first month he was there, Rob just played it cool. Got his feet wet. Figured out how things worked. One of the people who taught him the ropes was Jack Layton. Even back in 2000, Jack was a seasoned political veteran.

"I learned the ins and outs from Jack," Rob told me. "And whenever it came to voting on something, I'd just look at Jack, and whichever way he was gonna vote, I'd vote the opposite."

This was both funny and true, but Rob didn't mean it without some genuine affection. In fact, Rob loved Jack Layton. Even though they had their political differences, they still got along very well. Rob never really cared about political party allegiances. He just liked the common folk that he could sit down and relate to, and Jack had a real down-to-earth, human side that appealed to Rob.

Right from the get-go, Rob understood that the issue at city hall was spending, not revenue. Spending, and a serious sense of entitlement to go with it. He wasn't afraid to speak his mind in committee meetings and in the council chamber. It made him lots of enemies and few friends, but he didn't care about that. He cared about doing the right thing. And if that meant getting in a few people's faces, so be it. This was the same Rob who'd played tough industrial-league hockey with me. This Rob was a fighter.

(For my part, I didn't really understand what was going on. I was in Chicago a lot of the time, focusing on our new Deco branch down there, so I was pretty removed. Rob would call me and say, "Jones, you wouldn't believe what's happening. They're all a bunch of crooks here." I believed him, but I couldn't really comprehend it for myself until I got to city hall and saw the extent of the problems first-hand.)

One of the very first fights Rob threw himself into was over the city budget. Things were out of control, and Toronto was looking at a major tax increase to cover the costs. But Rob wasn't having it. The first thing he stood up against was an increase in property taxes. That was back in 2001, and of course he was one of the only councillors who had the guts to vote against the motion. He was devoted, even then, to protecting the taxpayer as much as possible. And if that wasn't enough to make his mark, he then took the fight to each councillor's expense account, rightfully pointing out how much taxpayer money was being wasted on trips and meals and other perks. The best part was, Rob led by example. He barely spent a penny of his own office budget, even through his first couple years in the seat (not even $20 all told). All his expenses—for essential things like stationery—came out of his own pocket. When council's annual expense reports were published, the other councillors started to fear what Rob's report would show (all zeroes, for the most part) and how their own reports would look in comparison.

Most of the time, Rob preferred to spend his days in his ward, just doing his constituent calls and staying away from the drama of the council chamber. People would call him and, much to their surprise, Rob would return the call. He'd often even show up at their door, almost by the time they'd hung up, because it's a relatively small area to cover. He was *always* on the side of his constituents. He'd taken our dad's approach to customer service and put his own spin on it, and what he'd come up with were two rules. Rule number one: the customer—or in this case, the constituent—is always right. Rule number two: refer back to rule number one.

It didn't take long for Rob's dedication to his constituents to build him a strong reputation. That's when the calls from outside his ward started to come in. And not surprisingly, he responded to those calls the same way as he did in Etobicoke North. It didn't matter to him where they were coming from—he'd go anywhere in the city to lend a hand. Sure enough, a number of the other councillors didn't like this. It was making them look bad, especially when it was their own constituents calling Rob for help. It had always been too easy for councillors and city staff to just shrug a problem off and say they couldn't do anything about it. Rob hated hearing that. It was unacceptable to him. If a constituent had a problem and the city staff were saying they couldn't fix it, Rob would fix it himself. I used to joke with him that even if it was a cat stuck up in a tree, Rob would try to climb up there to get that cat. He didn't even keep a constituency office. His office, he said, was meeting people at their front doors.

CHAPTER 10

Second Term

Rob's first term as a councillor came to an end in the middle of 2003, when Toronto voters went to the polls again. Rob's old seat-neighbour, Jack Layton, had moved on to take the lead of the federal NDP. And back in January of that year, Mel Lastman had said he wasn't going to seek re-election, so a whole new pool of mayoral contenders put their names in. The favourite (at first, anyway) was Lastman's old rival, Barbara Hall. There were also John Nunziata, John Tory and David Miller. Barbara Hall couldn't maintain a campaign, and before long, the race was really just between Tory and Miller. In the end, David Miller won. In my opinion, it was his appeal to the downtown lefties that handed him the mayoralty. For the time being, John Tory moved on to lead the provincial PC Party for the next four years.

In fact, we ended up meeting with John Tory. He called us to ask for our family's support in Etobicoke as he was making his move into provincial politics. We met him on Dixon Road at the board of trade office. Rob and I went, along with our mom and dad, and since Tory was a conservative, we told him we would support him. It's funny, because the media has made this out to be some kind of secret meeting. It wasn't anything of the sort. It was John Tory having lunch with a family who was well connected in the business community. I'm sure he met with dozens of other families and individuals the same way he'd sat down with us. But I suppose that doesn't make for an interesting or mysterious story.

It's also worth saying that Rob and David Miller always got along. They had two very different theories on politics. David, God bless him, had a very left-wing agenda, but it's what he believed in. On top of that, David was an honest politician. One of the very few. As a matter of fact, David came to visit Rob in the hospital before he passed away. I know Rob appreciated it, and it's also something I'll never forget.

In any case, Rob wasn't ready to run for mayor in 2003, but he was more than happy to try his luck as a councillor again. During his first term on council, he'd only scratched the surface of all the financial mismanagement at city hall, and he was ready to take it all on in an even bigger way.

I helped him campaign again, and it was nothing new—we just got out there, knocked on the doors, put up the signs and talked to the voters. On election night, Rob finished with over 10,000 votes—an 80 percent landslide for Etobicoke North.

Rob's life wasn't just defined by his job as a councillor; my brother had a lot of things going on outside city hall as well. By the time he entered his second term representing Etobicoke North, he'd been married for a couple of years. Rob had a few girlfriends throughout high school and into university, but nothing serious. He knew Renata Brejniak from Scarlett Heights; she also lived a couple of blocks away from us. Renata came and worked at Deco for a year after she graduated from high school. That's how Rob really got to know her—when he came home from university and worked at Deco too—and before long, they were dating.

They got married in 2000, after Rob's first election victory. The wedding was held at All Saints, a Catholic church on Royal York Road. We'd grown up in the United Church, and we were pretty easygoing about religion overall, but it was very important to Renata's parents, Henryka and Tadeusz, that their daughter and son-in-law be married in a Catholic ceremony. It wasn't a huge wedding, with not more than 100 guests. I was the best man. We had the reception at St. George's Golf and Country Club.

Rob and Renata's daughter, Stephanie, would be born in 2005, and Dougie would come along in 2007. As Rob's political career started to pick up some real momentum, Renata transitioned into a full-time stay-at-home mom. I mention this because I think it's important to understand the other side of Rob. He had already set himself apart at city hall by being an honest, scrappy councillor who didn't care what others thought of him so long as he was protecting the taxpayer, but it's easy to forget that he was also a family man. A husband and a dad. A brother and a son. This is what I believe John Tory meant when he remembered my brother as a "profoundly human guy."[1] I also think this was easy for a lot of Rob's detractors to forget or ignore.

For Rob's part, I don't think he ever forgot about the human side of the councillors he was taking on. He'd made his enemies pretty quickly, especially among the lefties, but he also understood that politics is a lot of theatrics. The vast majority of those councillors didn't get much airtime, so they'd put on a big show in council meetings—screaming, yelling, all the rest. We even had a few councillors and city staff attend Ford Fest and our family barbecues over the years. John Tory, David Miller and many of the others were in our backyard at one time or another. When it came to life outside city hall, Rob's big heart always shone through.

Nowhere was this more evident than his football coaching at various high schools in the west end of Toronto. After he'd come back to the city in the early 1990s, Rob had volunteered as a football coach at Scarlett Heights, our old high school. From there, he moved on to Newtonbrook Secondary up in North York, and then to Don Bosco Catholic Secondary School. The amount of time, energy and even money that Rob put into his coaching still amazes me. Sure enough, he got criticized in the council chamber for missing the odd vote or debate during the fall when he was out coaching his team on weekday afternoons, but there is just no way of understating what he was doing for those young people. Many of them came from tough neighbourhoods and tough backgrounds. (Rob got in trouble for talking about this very thing.) Rob worked them hard on the field, but he also took good care of them, mentoring them and writing countless letters of reference for jobs.

ROB'S SECOND TERM as a councillor was not much different from his first. He spent as much time as he could in his ward, taking care of his constituents' problems. Back at city hall, it was more of the same for him too as he took on the spending and the entitlements and the perks. What really launched Rob's popularity was *The John Oakley*

Show on AM640. Rob was invited to go on the show every Thursday at 8:00 a.m. Rob had developed a bit of a reputation by then for his straight-up opinions and style, and Oakley wanted to hear more from him. So here came Rob on a regular basis now, blowing the whistle about all the scandals and exotic lunches and ridiculous travel expenses and everything else. The gravy train, basically. Rob called it all out on Oakley's show. That's usually unheard of—a politician calling out his colleagues like that—but Rob was a lone wolf. And Oakley and his listeners loved it. While many Toronto residents had no idea who their own councillor might be, they were all starting to know who Rob was.

It didn't feel like very long before 2006, another election year, arrived. This time around, the provincial government passed legislation that extended municipal terms from three years to four, so Rob could expect to represent Etobicoke North until 2010. He wasn't considering a run for the mayoralty in 2006, despite some promises he'd made in the heat of a debate. I think Rob wanted to see what David Miller would do with another term, even though the city budget was turning into a runaway horse.

I'm no fan of the *Toronto Star*, but it amuses me to see how even that liberal rag was criticizing city council's spending habits. In a 2007 article, Royson James talked about how a number of councillors—Cesar Palacio, Joe

Mihevc and Sandra Bussin, among others—claimed more than $50,000 in expenses for the fiscal year. Doug Holyday, meanwhile, had kept his expenses to a little over $1,000. Last, but not least, was Rob, who did not spend a single penny of his budget for 2007. James also talked about how some councillors even went after Rob and Doug Holyday for their fiscal responsibility—a move that backfired in the eyes of the taxpayers and only caused more embarrassment for the rest of council. This was all coming out in the *Toronto Star*, which should prove how ridiculous things had become.[2]

In any case, Rob campaigned in Etobicoke North the same way he had twice before, and he easily reclaimed his seat on election night in November 2006. Although it was another win for Rob, none of us felt much like celebrating: Dad had passed away only a month and a half earlier, and our family was still feeling the big hole he'd left behind.

Between Dad's passing and the attacks on Rob (usually about how minimal his expenses were or how he was coaching high school football) from some of the other councillors at city hall, I know Rob's third term was a lonely time. But as those four years passed, Rob had a lot to be proud of. One of his major accomplishments was finally changing that culture of entitlement at city hall. Once Rob got on John Oakley's show, he really started holding people accountable and calling them out. The councillors in his sights might not have paid him much attention at first, but what they didn't understand was that there were hundreds of thousands of listeners across the Greater Toronto Area agreeing with him. Finally, in 2008, council passed a new expense policy that cracked down hard on mileage, meals and alcohol.[3] It didn't go nearly far enough, but it was a start, and Rob rightly felt proud of it.

The other thing Rob accomplished was maintaining customer service. He never deviated from it. As I talked about before, Etobicoke North was the new home for thousands of people from around the world. Some of those countries are places riddled with corruption at all levels of government, and the folks coming from those places know it when they see it—even if it's the kind of polished up, minor mismanagement going on at Toronto City Hall. So between Rob's dedication to returning phone calls or visiting his constituents, and publicly calling out his fellow councillors for their financial mismanagement, the people in his ward knew he'd given them a voice.

Meanwhile, David Miller's mayoralty was in bad shape. The land transfer and vehicle registration taxes he'd come up with were hugely unpopular. City spending had risen to almost $9 billion a year by 2009, leaving a shortfall of up to $500 million and a huge road-repair backlog.[4] Then there was the 2009 garbage strike—over a month of suspended pickup services, during which places like

Christie Pits ended up as temporary dumping grounds. That strike was the nail in David Miller's political coffin. In September of that year, Miller told the city he wouldn't run for re-election.

It's worth saying that I fully believe David Miller is an honest man and was an honest mayor, despite our differences in political beliefs. There was one major obstacle for Miller, and it was the same obstacle Rob faced, as did Mel Lastman, as did any other mayor of Toronto. That obstacle was the councillors. As Miller said, it wasn't the job that wore him down, it was fighting with council. Even his own team, the lefties, constantly got in his way and made Toronto's city hall the most dysfunctional political arena in the country. Part of the reason for this is that 44 councillors are, in effect, 44 independent contractors. They have no allegiance to anyone. There's no party, per se, like you have in municipal politics in the US, so it's just a free-for-all, with each one of these independent contractors pushing their own agenda.

If I ever get to the provincial level of politics, municipal affairs is the first thing I would want to change. I think mayors across this province deserve stronger powers. One person in charge, with veto power, similar to the strong mayoral systems in New York and Chicago and LA. I would want our mayors to have strong powers but to be held accountable; if the voters don't like the job he or she is doing, they can fire that mayor in four years. That's how it should work.

I don't know if there was any one thing in particular that pushed Rob into the decision to run for mayor, but I do know that he'd had enough of all the craziness. He'd decided the time had come to fix things the way he believed they should be fixed. What I didn't know yet is that I was going to city hall with him.

CHAPTER 11

Doug

Doug Ford often refers to the city in company terms. He's had bottom lines on the brain since he was seven years old. Back then he was calculating income from his Globe and Mail *paper route. "Those Saturday papers, I tell you, those were killers."*[1]

—*The Globe and Mail*, June 11, 2011

My brother never thought of himself as a politician. Neither did my dad. And neither do I. I'm a family man, first and foremost, but my calling through most of my adult life has been leading the Ford family business into the next generation. I'm proud of being an independent Canadian business leader, and there are few things I love as much as the challenge of sales. I'm saying this because these are the unique experiences that I brought to politics when I went to city hall with Rob in

2010. This is Rob's story overall, but I want to talk a little bit about how I ended up where I am—and how I believe I was able to help my brother when so many other people were out to get him right from the beginning.

For starters, I never finished college. I don't regret that at all, but I think about it sometimes, and whenever I give speeches to high school students, I like to encourage them to think outside of going to university. Don't get me wrong—university is a critical experience for those who can do it. But that's not everybody. Looking at a high school audience, I know some kids are sitting there thinking, "My God, where am I going next?" For those young people, I always like to tell a few stories. For instance, even if you cut lawns—maybe as a summer job in your neighbourhood—if you go knock on some doors, get yourself 12 customers, all of a sudden, you're in the lawn-care business. Or you can be a house painter. Or you can get a trade, maybe become a carpenter. These days, good carpenters make $100,000 a year. So I explain to high school audiences that not everybody needs to be an academic. The main thing is, whatever you do, you just have to stay focused and don't give up.

For me, working has been a part of my life for almost as long as I can remember—just as it was for Rob as well. I helped out at Deco all through my childhood, but when I was 14, the summer after I finished Grade 8, I moved to my maternal grandparents' two-bedroom apartment out at Victoria Park and Ellesmere. I moved in with them because my aunt had got me a job at a place called Security Credit. Security Credit manufactured credit cards. They paid me $3.50 an hour. I would mainly help laminate the cards. They got printed on a big sheet of paper, then a piece of Mylar would be put on the bottom and top, and the whole thing would be sandwiched together in an oven. My dad was only paying me $3 an hour to work at Deco, so for that extra 50 cents, plus the opportunity to learn something new, I went and lived with my grandparents, Clarence and Mabel Campbell. I'd leave their house at six in the morning, hop on the bus and go all the way up Victoria Park, past Steeles Avenue, to the south end of Markham, where Security Credit was located. The building itself had very high security, which was pretty interesting for a boy of 14.

My last scheduled day of work that summer was a Friday. Grade 9 was just around the corner. I got up early as usual. My grandfather Clarence got up at the same time, but there was something weird about him that day. "Call 9-1-1," he told me. So I called 9-1-1. A little while later, the ambulance arrived and took him away. I didn't know what else to do, so I still went to work. Before the day was over, my grandfather had passed away, and that was how my summer working at Security Credit ended.

Through my high school years, I worked at Canada Packers, a meat-packing plant in the St. Clair and Keele area of Toronto. Canada Packers later went on to be amalgamated into Maple Leaf Foods. I made $12.49 an hour and I still feel like that was the best job I ever had, outside of what I'm doing now. I started there when I was 16, in Grade 10. Originally, it was my friend's idea to apply. He asked me to give him a lift, so I took him in my old Firebird. We both walked into the human resources office, and to my surprise, the head of Canada Packers HR was the mother of a girl I went to school with. (As a funny coincidence, that same girl I knew from school went on to hire my daughter at Royal LePage a few years ago.) Anyway, the head of HR offered my friend a job, and me along with him. Canada Packers was hiring a bunch of high school guys at the time because it was heavy labour—perfect for young men like us. I didn't know what to make of it at first, but I did know that $12.49 an hour sounded a lot better than anything else I was doing!

On Saturdays, we would load sides of beef from 7:00 a.m. until 3:30 p.m. We would all partner up. One guy would load boxes of meat onto a conveyor belt, and the other guy would take the boxes off the belt and hand-pack them into a 53-foot reefer trailer. If you were the guy packing the trailer, you'd pack 30,000 kilograms of boxes by yourself. On Sunday nights, we started at 7:00 p.m.

and worked until the work was finished. There would be a team of four or five of us. The sides of beef, about 300 pounds each, would come down from the slaughterhouse, which was at the top of the building. Two or three guys on the team would carry the side of beef, one guy would cut it, one guy would tie it, and then the carrier would shoot the beef down the rails in the truck. We would go all night like that, but for some reason, I found Sunday nights easier than Saturday shifts. Either way, it kept us all in great shape. We were also able to work a few shifts on weeknights, but since we were all part-timers, we couldn't exceed more than 24 hours total in a week, as some kind of deal with the meat-packers' union. But that was okay—24 hours a week still meant just shy of $300 in my pocket, which was a lot of money back then, especially for a high school student, even though I'd be bagged getting to school in the morning after a night shift. As it turned out, my friend whom I'd been hired on with only lasted a month or so, but I really loved it at Canada Packers, and I stayed on for the rest of my high school years.

Outside of Canada Packers, there was school to think about. Grade 13 was drawing to a close for me. I knew I didn't have the marks for university, like many of the kids in the audiences I speak to today. At that time, I had to make some decisions about the future. I'd always loved playing sports, and I did get a couple of letters from the coaches at Mount Allison and Acadia encouraging me to play football at their schools, out on the East Coast. But even back then, I didn't want to leave Toronto. I've always been a homeboy. This is where I wanted to stay. I was interested in getting more involved with Deco, our family business, so in the meantime, I enrolled in a business administration diploma course at Humber College.

In September 1984, I started my first year of college. Right from the start, I didn't think it was for me. I was bored silly in the lectures, and there were no varsity sports at Humber back then. All in all, college was pretty disappointing after how much I'd loved high school. But as it turned out, it wasn't a problem for very long. One day in October of my first year, I went to campus only to find all my classes were cancelled. The teachers had all gone on strike. This wasn't just at Humber; the teachers at every college in Ontario had gone on strike, protesting contract offers they weren't happy with. The strike would go on for almost a month. A lot of students got involved by staging protests at Queen's Park in an attempt to force negotiations, but for me, this was a much different turning point. The day I got to campus only to find the classes cancelled, I turned around and went straight back home. Then I put on a suit and tie and drove up to Deco.

Back then, before we'd put the addition on the building, Deco was just 10,000 square feet, so I knew it wouldn't be long before my dad spotted me. Sure enough, as soon as he saw me, he wanted to know what was going on.

"The teachers are on strike," I said. "So I just want to work here in sales for now."

Dad frowned at me. "Just so we're clear," he said, "there's no way you're quitting school. You're going to go back after the strike."

Then Dad took me out to do some cold calls. The first one I remember was at a commercial office building at York Mills and Don Mills.

"Okay," said Dad. "Start dropping off brochures."

So that's how it started for me. I went up and down the stairs of that building, into each company's front office, dropping off our brochures, getting the names and phone numbers of each company's purchasing agent. Before long, we'd both worked up a sweat from all the trips up and down the stairs, but from the very beginning, I loved the challenge of the cold call. I loved being able to go out and sell a good product and offer people a service they might otherwise not be getting.

I think part of the reason I loved it so much was that I believed in what we did. Labelling has always been a special service. Every product in the world has a label on it, and in turn, I believe every household in North America has one of Deco's labels under the hood of their car, in their medicine cabinet, on their cosmetics or in their fridge. Very few industries are that diversified, so we get the pulse of the economy. When we're selling labels, that means manufacturers are selling their products, even if it's a shipping label. And I still do cold calls almost every day. I call companies anywhere in North America and give them our pitch and hopefully can get an appointment. I like to drive past office buildings in this city, knowing I've gone in there and at least made an effort to drop a brochure off and make some contacts.

That first day, back in 1984, was the only time Dad went out with me, but I took to it like a duck to water. I had told him I'd go back to Humber after the strike, but I think I already knew my time at college was over. I learned more about business in those first 30 days of cold-calling than I ever did in a classroom.

Not long after I started my career in sales, I met a woman at one of our family's big backyard barbecues. It wasn't uncommon for there to be a couple hundred people or more at these barbecues. I'd never seen her before. I introduced myself to her. Her name was Karla Middlebrook. She'd grown up in Etobicoke and was working as a showroom model at a bridal shop downtown. I hadn't really thought about dating at that time. I wanted to get established and make sure Deco was moving forward.

Still, there was something different about Karla Middlebrook. Something I couldn't ignore. We started dating, and two years later Karla came on board at Deco in customer service. Over the next couple of years, we got more and more serious, and on November 12, 1988, we were married. It was a wedding of about 200 people. We held it at the Old Mill and it cost about $12,000. We paid for it ourselves. Rob was my best man.

At first, Karla and I moved to Brampton because we couldn't afford a place in Toronto. Our place in Brampton was a condo, for which we paid about $150,000. Then, in 1990, the so-called real estate bubble throughout the Greater Toronto Area popped; we sold our condo and lost $50,000. From that day forward, my opinion has been that condos are one of the worst investments a person can make. I see the same thing happening nowadays—this crazily booming condo market (not just in the GTA but in Vancouver and other parts of Canada as well)—and I can't help but feel the bubble is bound to pop again.

Anyway, we ended up back in Etobicoke, in a house on Tynevale Drive for five years, and then finally to the house in Princess Anne Manor. We're still there to this day. Maybe it had something to do with moving out of a condo and back into the neighbourhood where Karla and I had grown up, but things happened pretty quickly after that—

we had four daughters in five years. The first was Krista, followed by Kayla, Kara and Kyla. After Kayla was born, my wife quit her job at Deco to be a stay-at-home mom, which of course is a full-time job in its own right.

CHAPTER 12

Chicago Calling

As soon as my daughters could walk, they were all into sports, which obviously made me pretty happy. I coached their T-ball and soccer teams, but I'll admit that it was a tough balance with how hard I was working at Deco. I was, without question, a workaholic. On one hand, I wanted to be more involved in their lives. On the other hand, I knew I was going to have to expand the business in order to take care of my family.

This, I believe, was one of the main reasons why I wanted to take Deco into the US. Initially, Dad advised against it. "Don't worry about the US," he told me. "Focus on Toronto." That plan might've worked for him, but I had a sense of the massive market in the US. We'd been going every year to a printing trade show—Labelexpo—based in Chicago. Chicago was the printing hub of the US, and people at the trade show would tell me, "Oh, it's a tough market here." I became attracted to expanding there, because if it was a tough market, and so many other printing companies were based out of Chicago, then there had to be a tremendous amount of business there.

So on New Year's Eve, 1998, I asked our accountant, a British man named John Lahey, to come down to Chicago with me. I never even told my dad what I was doing, but John and I flew down together first thing on New Year's Day. We met with a real estate agent, an aggressive young Romanian-American woman, the only person I'd contacted who was willing to wake up on New Year's Day and show John and me around. We looked mainly in the Chicago suburbs, and the name of one suburb in particular kept popping up: Elk Grove Village.

Elk Grove Village is the largest industrial park in North America. It's near O'Hare International Airport, is serviced by several major highways and is home to almost 4,000 businesses. It didn't take me long to realize we were in the perfect location for what I wanted to achieve. We ended up finding a tiny office of not much more than 1,000 square feet. It cost $1,100 a month. I asked John if we could afford it, plus a start-up investment of $80,000 or so to get us going. John assured me that we could, so I signed the lease on the spot.

John headed back to Toronto as soon as the lease was

signed, but I stayed. I remember how I sat there, in that empty office in Chicago, thinking, "Okay, I've got to start a business now." And all I could do was go back to my early sales experience—that very first day when Dad and I went to York Mills and Don Mills—and start cold calling.

It took 10 months to get things going in Chicago. I shipped some printing equipment and desks down, and hired a small office staff mainly to watch the phones. My dad still thought it was a crazy idea, but I never lost faith that it would work out. The US is all about opportunity and prosperity, if you're willing to stick it out and put in the hard work, and that's what I was doing.

Our first big contract in the US was printing labels for CLR, the cleaning solution. The CFO of CLR was Canadian. He grew up around Weston Road, actually, so even though he'd relocated to the US, he and I hit it off as soon as we met. I'm still grateful for the business he gave us. By October, I was able to bring on three salesmen—they're still with us today—and we moved four times in five years to increasingly larger facilities.

It didn't take long to realize Chicago was the right move for us, and Deco's profitability overall really started to climb. I'd go down every week to make calls and send out brochures.

The early 2000s were a good time for our family. My dad was enjoying retirement—well, as close to retirement as he ever got—and Rob was into his first and then second term as a city councillor and was already making a name for himself. His own kids, Stephanie and Dougie, came along in 2005 and 2007 respectively. It was close to the time we lost our dad, but we felt grateful to have a healthy new generation of our family.

In 2008, I undertook Deco's next expansion. This was into New Jersey, which was another vibrant—and somewhat untapped—market. This expansion was the most challenging thing I'd ever done in my life. We bought out a bankrupt label company. They had a big place, 60,000 square feet. We rightsized the operation. Our New Jersey division was barely up and running before a bunch of creditors from that company's former days came out of the woodwork, looking for money. Getting that all sorted out was an absolute nightmare. If I had to do it over again, I don't think I would've bought out that business; I just would've started from scratch.

Anyhow, in spite of the difficulties getting going, and in spite of all the time I had to spend away from my family, I've never regretted a minute of the time I've spent building and running a successful business. I didn't finish college, but I learned invaluable lessons. I learned not to bullshit anybody and not to pull punches. I learned customer service, how to run a profitable operation, and how to create jobs for people. By 2009, with Chicago and Toronto turning millions of dollars in revenue, and New Jersey up and running, I wasn't completely sure what the next step would be. I was thinking of more expansion throughout the US. I definitely wasn't thinking about politics—not as far as my own fate was concerned, anyway.

CHAPTER 13

The Once and Future Mayor

In the end the ballot question became: Ford, yes or no? On Monday night, Toronto's electorate overwhelmingly voted yes.[1]

—*The Globe and Mail*, October 25, 2010

It was January of 2010, and I was down at Deco's Chicago office. I wasn't thinking about Toronto at all, really . . . until one day in the office, my phone rang, and when I picked it up, Rob was on the other end.

"Jones," said Rob, "did you hear? John Tory's not running for mayor."

This came as a pretty big surprise. With David Miller stepping out of the picture, everyone thought John Tory was going to take a run at the mayoralty. Tory was the establishment guy. But he apparently wanted to focus on his Newstalk 1010 radio show and his involvement with a civic advocacy group called Toronto City Summit Alliance. With Tory out of the picture, that left a bit more of an open race. There had been talk that Joe Pantalone might make a run at it, as well as Karen Stintz and Rocco Rossi and even Giorgio Mammoliti. The biggest name being tossed around was Ontario's deputy premier, George Smitherman.

"I'm gonna jump in there," said Rob.

I grinned when I heard this. I wasn't surprised—I knew Rob's taking a chance at the seat had been pretty much inevitable for a long time—but it was still good to hear him say it. Not that I didn't think it was going to be a tough fight. Rob was the outsider, standing against a strong political establishment. But I knew he had the pulse of the taxpayers, the average Joes, the common people of every stripe.

"I'll come home right away," I told him. "Count me in for the campaign. Whatever you need."

"I need more than your help," said Rob. "I need you to run in my seat."

I laughed. "I'll help you," I said, "but there's no way *I'm* running."

For the moment, we left it at that. As far as my brother's political career went, I was more than happy to help him in any way I could. Between my dad's, Doug Holyday's and Rob's own early campaigns over the years, I'd learned a few tricks of the trade. But to run myself, for the circus that was Toronto city council? No way. That just wasn't in the cards for me.

Or so I thought.

ROB PUBLICLY ANNOUNCED his campaign on *The John Oakley Show* on AM640. It was late March, and even though this was Rob's regular radio spot, we still made a bit of a show of it. We rented a bus, grabbed a whole bunch of people, made up some signs and turned the whole thing into a celebration. The next night, we did an official kickoff at the Toronto Congress Centre back home in Etobicoke. A few thousand people showed up to offer their support. Jim Flaherty was there with his wife, MPP Christine Elliott (the only elected Conservatives in the country to show up). A number of Rob's football players and their families also came out. It was the first of many rock-star moments for Rob. I found myself a little overwhelmed by the crowd's response to my brother. I knew he was on to something, but I didn't know *how* positive the response was going to be, right from the outset.

The mainstream media, of course, wanted to imply that Rob didn't stand a chance. The smart money, it seemed, was on George Smitherman, especially with John Tory out of the race. Smitherman was coming from the provincial government and already had the overt support of the Ontario Liberal Party. He was also backed by a number of lefty councillors. Sarah Thomson even suspended her bid for mayor to back Smitherman's campaign. But in Rob's opinion, Smitherman was the most incompetent politician around. Never mind all the stuff about "Furious George" (the nickname the press gave Smitherman for his aggressive attitude); Smitherman had been the provincial minister of health and long-term care when much of the eHealth boondoggle went down. Almost a billion dollars in untendered contracts and CEO bonuses was wasted—enough that Smitherman's successor, David Caplan, had to resign once the public got wind of it all.[2]

In any case, Smitherman had announced his candidacy for mayor back in November of 2009. The other well-known candidates included Rocco Rossi, who'd been working as national director of the federal Liberals and CEO of the Heart and Stroke Foundation, as well as Giorgio Mammoliti, Joe Pantalone and Adam Giambrone. The latter three were all Rob's fellow councillors from city hall. Giambrone, a favourite among the lefties, was serving as the chair of the TTC at the time, which already made him unpopular, given a recent fare hike, but his campaign for the mayoralty fell apart pretty quickly after an affair he was having with a university student came to light.[3] He was forced to make a public apology. A couple days later, he dropped out of the race.

As for Rob's campaign, we knew we had a battle ahead of us, so there was no time to lose in crafting a strategy. We had our first campaign meeting in the basement of our family house on Weston Wood, and this was where I first met some of the folks who'd be part of Rob's story over the next couple of years—for better or for worse. One of those people was a consultant named Mark Towhey. I'm not sure how he'd ended up at that basement meeting, but he seemed pretty sharp and ready to get to work. On top of that, he was from south Etobicoke, so right there was a point in his favour. His organizational sense and book smarts made him a good fit for the position of assistant campaign manager. My own role, I guess, could be called campaign "chair"; I was helping out with everything.

As far as a strategy went, we wanted to focus on grass-roots issues that were important to voters all across the city. City hall's financial screw-ups were the biggest issues on people's minds, so we settled on a theme of respecting the taxpayer and, more famously, "stopping the gravy train." This was something Rob had talked about over and over as a councillor; now it worked perfectly as a campaign slogan.

Another aspect of our strategy was to use Rob's appeal to common people all across the city. In fact, we had a bit of a secret weapon. It sounds a lot more dramatic than it really was. The secret weapon was the records Rob had kept of all the people he'd visited and calls he'd returned as a councillor over the years. Rob had boxes and boxes full of 8.5-by-11-inch sheets of paper, and on these sheets of paper were columns of phone numbers. Just numbers. No names, no addresses. Rob had kept these numbers over the years, and there had to be tens of thousands of them.

I remember calling Rob once and saying, "Rob, where are you?" This was before he was mayor, and it was during the 2009 garbage strike.

Rob said, "I'm on Kingston Road in Scarborough [well outside of his ward]. I'm picking up Mrs. Johnson's garbage. She's a widow. She's 70 years old and she can't get to the garbage dump."

I have no idea who Mrs. Johnson was. I don't know if she'd been a lifelong NDP voter, or Green, Liberal or Conservative. It didn't matter. That one personal visit Rob had made, the way he'd helped her out, and the fact that he'd then recorded her phone number on one of these sheets of paper, gave us a strategic edge when it came to our campaign. Because all we had to do was start going down the list and making calls. That's what the media and the elites and the political establishment just did not understand about Rob.

To simultaneously reach out to Rob's supporters all across Toronto—to make use of our secret weapon, in other words—we would need to do something that had never been done before in Canadian politics. This was where a small polling and data service company called Campaign Research came in handy. Campaign Research had a specialized, cutting-edge telephone outreach system that would work perfectly for what we wanted to do.

As a matter of fact, Campaign Research's two founding partners, Nick Kouvalis and Richard Ciano, had made contact with us. They were both conservatives and were interested in what Rob was bringing to the race. When we met them, Nick Kouvalis struck us as a bit of a rough-around-the-edges guy, while Richard Ciano was a little more slick and polished. We hired them on. Initially, Ciano took the post of strategy adviser and campaign manager, but it didn't take long for us all to realize it wasn't the best match personality-wise. So we switched the roster up and gave the bulk of the job to Kouvalis. This was his first mayoral campaign, and he worked very hard at it—even if he and I had our differences later on. In any case, I believe we were the first campaign in Canada to do telephone town halls, but they let Rob reach out to tens of thousands of people at a time and conduct a two-way conversation with them. This was another strategic edge.

In order to manage the communications part of our campaign, we brought on a woman named Adrienne Batra. Initially, we'd wanted conservative journalist Tasha Kheiriddin to come aboard in the communications role, but Tasha was on maternity leave when we contacted her. She said to us, "I can't do it, but there's someone from out West you might like." The person Kheiriddin was referring to was Batra, who was working with the Canadian Taxpayers Federation in Winnipeg. Batra had recently moved to Toronto. She was happy to come aboard as our communications adviser. Batra did a great job for us. She was funny and sharp and watched out for Rob on the campaign trail. (After Rob won the election, Batra took on the job of his press secretary at city hall. In late 2011, she got a job offer over at the *Toronto Sun*. We were very sorry to see her go, but it was a great opportunity for her. Batra is still there now, serving as editor-in-chief.)

Rob certainly wasn't a typical candidate for Batra, Kouvalis and Towhey to work with. We believed in lots of signs and big rallies for our base. That's what Ford Fest turned into during the campaign season. I've seen Donald Trump doing similar rallies (although much bigger in scale) in his campaign, but we were doing it long before he was. We campaigned hard right through spring and summer and into the fall, all of September and October. All of my efforts were with Rob, supporting his run. It was going to be a fight, and we knew it. Never mind the other candidates—the media had already set their sights on us, and in some ways, I think they were our worst enemy, right from day one.

The *Toronto Star* ran a front-page story reporting on a confrontation Rob had with one of the kids he coached in football. Two unnamed sources, a player and a parent, claimed Rob had physically accosted the student. Other sources said the altercation was only verbal. A couple of weeks later, the kid, whose name was Jonathan Gordon, was interviewed by *The Globe and Mail*. He'd grown into a young man, had joined the military and was serving at Canadian Forces Base Trenton. Jonathan told *The Globe* that Rob "never laid a hand on him."[4] Rob was a tough football coach, for sure, but he loved those kids. He hated that people reading that *Star* story could think differently.

It didn't stop with the football story, either. The media started digging into his past. Toward the end of the campaign, a story came out about Rob getting busted for a DUI and for having a joint down in Florida, way back in the 1990s. When it happened, Rob had pleaded guilty. In other words, he'd been truthful and owned up to it, and the charge for pot was eventually dropped, and everyone got on with their lives. Anyway, fast forward to 2010, and I believe the *Toronto Sun* ran the story first, but within a few days, everybody else—the *Star*, *The Globe*, the CBC—ran it too.

When the joint story hit, I thought Rob was finished. I guess the media thought so too. At our campaign office, the telephone lines were lighting up like a Christmas tree. But when asked for comment, Rob did the same thing he'd done when he'd been caught with the joint 11 years earlier: he just owned up to it and admitted his mistake. And sure enough, the next day, he was polling better than ever. This was happening because he was *real*. He was an *average guy*. The story about the joint just proved it, and in turn it was a complete backfire for the media who seemed intent on bringing him down.

It's funny, because I think if you look at the media's relationship with the mayor now, it's a lot different. In my opinion, that has a lot to do with the fact that the mayor (at the time of writing) is John Tory. I've known him for a long time. I believe John Tory, like David Miller, is honest. But at the same time, I feel as if there are a lot of developers and elites that have surrounded him; they're good at pressuring him for what they want, and John Tory is too nice of a guy to say no. He wants to be good friends with everyone; he has no political will and, in my opinion, dithers too much when it comes to decision making.

By mid-summer in 2010, Giorgio Mammoliti had dropped out of the race. He'd only been polling in the single digits, and as a right-winger, his departure was a boon for Rob.[5] Rob's main opponents still included George Smitherman and Joe Pantalone, with Rocco Rossi starting to trail behind. For my part, I'd meant what I'd said to Rob about my intentions to stay out of the race. But one day Rob invited me to lunch at a Swiss Chalet on Victoria Park Avenue out in the east end. Joining us was Mike Del Grande, who'd been the councillor for Ward 39, Scarborough-Agincourt, since 2003. If the election went our way, Rob wanted to make Del Grande his budget chief.

At first, the three of us just talked about the progress of the campaign and some upcoming debates. Then Del Grande gave me a no-bullshit look and said, "Look, Doug, if your brother ends up as mayor, he's going to need your help. City hall is a wild place. He's going to need someone like you backing him up."

I sat back, not sure how to reply. In all honesty, this had occurred to me before. Rob and I had even talked about it a time or two, but it had always been at least somewhat easy to dismiss. Now, coming from someone like Del Grande, a seasoned councillor who understood what we were trying to do, I couldn't put the idea out of my mind so easily.

I dwelled on it for a few days. The campaign, meanwhile, was definitely heating up. Smitherman and his team had resorted to using a man in a chicken costume to try to goad Rob into a one-on-one debate, which we weren't interested in.[6] But it did make me realize what Rob would be up against, both during his campaign and as mayor. There would be an all-out effort to try to bring Rob down or throw him off his game.

Mike Del Grande, I realized, was right. More than that, *Rob* was right. He'd been right at the very beginning, when he'd called me in Chicago to tell me he was running and that I should take his seat in Etobicoke North.

So I talked to my wife, and I made the necessary arrangements at Deco to put some things on hold. Then in early August, during that year's Ford Fest barbecue in our backyard on Weston Wood, I announced that I'd be running too.

Looking back on it, I don't think anybody in our family was surprised. Everybody knew I couldn't let Rob go it alone.

The next business day, I paid my nomination fee, filled out the application and registered as a candidate. There were a few other candidates for the ward, but I didn't know any of them. I rented a storefront at Elmhurst Plaza, up near Islington and Rexdale Boulevard, and started my own campaign the same way I'd helped Doug Holyday and my dad with their campaigns—by knocking on doors. I didn't need to do that for very long, however. My dad had represented the area as an MPP, and Rob had represented it as a councillor for 10 years. People already knew us well and knew the kind of service we would give them. "Don't waste your time door-knocking here," people would tell me. "Help your brother get elected mayor."

* * *

SUMMER BECAME THE FALL, and election night drew closer. Rocco Rossi dropped out on October 13, leaving Smitherman, Pantalone and Rob as the contenders for mayor. Debates between Rob and Smitherman were particularly heated. Smitherman had the chicken-costume shtick to get under Rob's skin. Rob, on the other hand, only had to resort to presenting Smitherman's financial record. The eHealth boondoggle mostly under Smitherman's watch was exactly the kind of large-scale financial mismanagement that drove both Rob and the taxpayers crazy, and there was no way we were going to let Smitherman get away with it. We called it our "eHealth Hammer."

In debates, Smitherman's team wanted him to come across as slick and a quick talker, while Rob was just the average guy. We'd wait for Smitherman to get going about something in these debates, then we'd give Rob the nod. Rob would say, "You wasted almost a billion dollars of taxpayers' money on eHealth." If Smitherman tried to change the subject, Rob would repeat it over and over. The eHealth Hammer. George would go ballistic, get completely thrown off his game. It was a simple strategy for us, but it was true. It was a fair, accurate criticism of Smitherman's performance in politics, and he had nobody but himself to blame for it.

At the same time, Rob was more popular in the various ethnic communities around Toronto than any politician I can think of. They loved him because with Rob they actually had someone to call and speak to. All of a sudden, these new Canadians—many of whom had come from countries where the political scene is rotten with corruption—had a voice in local affairs. That was another thing George Smitherman simply underestimated.

We were moving ever closer to the end of October, and despite the best efforts of the media and the political establishment, Rob kept pulling ahead in the polls. By all accounts, he was unstoppable, and I felt overwhelmed by his momentum.

At the same time, George Smitherman was keeping up his fight. He believed his downtown fan club would be big enough to clinch the win. A few years later, Joe Pantalone told me a story about the election. He'd been contemplating stepping out of the race—this was in August—so he met with his campaign team, which consisted of about 20 people. Joe said to them, "If I decide to step down, how many people here would support George Smitherman?" No one raised their hands. "Okay, and how many people would vote for Rob Ford?" Everyone, every single one of them, raised their hands, Joe told me. And these were all NDP, union types. Smitherman definitely hadn't thought Rob would be popular with that demographic, but he was.

“The people are smart,” Rob would always say. “They know what they want.”

Well, he was right. The people knew what they wanted in 2010. They wanted Rob Ford to fix Toronto.

On October 25, 2010, the people of Toronto elected Rob Ford to be their new mayor.

DIANE FORD

When Doug Sr ran for provincial politics, Rob was really, really interested in the whole thing, as was Doug—in fact, Doug was instrumental in Doug Sr running. Doug Sr was in his mid-60s then, and he was a very successful businessman. That's what the PC Party was looking for. Doug was a strong conservative and was a rags-to-riches story—really a self-made man. All of this made a big impression on Rob. Also, Rob was definitely not a salesman like Doug Jr, but he loved helping people. That was his main passion.

As Rob's own political career started to get going, I said to him, "Why are you always spending so much time phoning everybody back?"

He said, "I know I'm helping them."

Rob also had his football foundation, where he helped so many kids. He had a good rapport with the teachers and the principals, and if any of his players missed school that day, they weren't allowed to practise or play. He always said to them, "School's your priority. Football's going to help you get along if you're really good, but education is what's going to take you through your life." He loved those kids, and they loved him.

When he was a brand new councillor, Rob took his dad and me on a tour of city hall. We went into the chamber. Council wasn't in session at the time, so nobody was there. I said, "Where are you going to sit, Rob?"

Our mom's favourite picture of us. *Left to right*: Rob and me at Al Ferri's apple farm in Brampton, fall 1973.

Young Rob Ford ready to dig into some cake. Note the gun rack in the corner, a real sign of the times. Our father, Doug Sr, was an avid hunter when we were kids.

Rob as a Cub Scout in the 1970s, working on his salute.

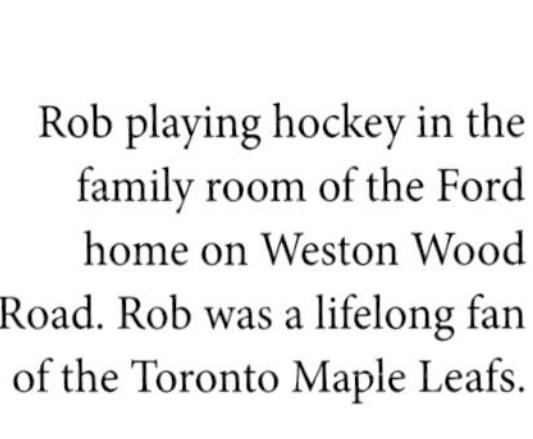

Rob playing hockey in the family room of the Ford home on Weston Wood Road. Rob was a lifelong fan of the Toronto Maple Leafs.

Rob joking around at Walt Disney World. Rob would later be pilloried in the press far worse than he was in this photo.

Rob in front of the White House in Washington, DC, 1986. I don't know if Rob had greater ambitions than being mayor of Toronto, but he sure had politics in his blood from an early age because of our dad's political career.

The Ford family in 1972. *Left to right*: Randy; Doug (in a bow tie); our mom, Diane; our dad, Doug Sr; Rob; and our sister, Kathy.

Rob and me at home on Weston Wood Road. I like to think Leafs fans would forgive Rob for wearing a Vancouver Canucks jersey.

Rob and our dad with Mohsine Hanafi (*right*), his mom and his brother, Zakaria, 1984. Mohsine, our Muslim brother from Morocco, came to stay with us as a student for a few days and ended up living with us for eight years.

Rob at 17 years old, in our family room. Growing up, Rob dreamed of becoming a professional football player and attended special camps for the Washington Redskins and Notre Dame.

Rob and our dad at Rob's high school graduation. Our father was a true inspiration for us, in business and in politics.

After graduating from Scarlett Heights Collegiate in Etobicoke, Rob studied at Carleton University before finding his way to the family business, Deco Labels and Tags, and, of course, to politics.

The Ford men at my wedding, November 12, 1989. *Left to right*: Randy, my dad, me and Rob, who was my best man.

Rob and Randy with the Conservative premier of Ontario at the time, Mike Harris. Our dad was one of the "Class of '95," key members of Mike Harris's team during the Common Sense Revolution.

Rob and Renata Brejniak with two of my daughters, Kara (*right*) and Kyla, 1998. Rob would marry Renata two years later and they would start a family of their own.

Rob with our mom and dad at Aventura Mall in Aventura, Florida, March 16, 1998. Our family has had a condo in Florida for many years, which offers some quiet time away from the maelstrom of Toronto politics.

At Rob and Renata's wedding, 2000. The reception was at St. George's Golf and Country Club on Islington Avenue in Etobicoke.

The family gathers at Rob's wedding. *Clockwise from lower left*: Me; Karla; Randy's girlfriend at the time, Lisa Dolson; our sister, Kathy; Randy; Kathy's son, Michael (*centre*); Dad; Mom; Rob; Renata; Kathy's daughter, Jennifer; and our four girls, Krista, Kayla, Kyla and Kara.

He said, "They haven't assigned a seat to me yet."

"So you have no idea where you're going to sit?" I said.

"Not right now," said Rob. But then he pointed at the mayor's seat and added, "But one day, I'm going to be sitting right up there."

When I think about it now, Rob had his sights on it. He really did.

Over the next few years, he spent a lot of time learning about how everything worked and what was going on at city hall. Then David Miller got voted in, and he was the other end of the spectrum completely. David was a nice man, but I think that's when Rob really made his mind up to run for mayor the next time around. By then, he had a lot of experience, and he could debate anybody. Rob had the courage of his convictions to keep him going. He also had his father in the background, even after Doug Sr passed away.

Then Rob became mayor, and Doug Jr got in as a councillor. A lot of the other councillors who were against them were all bleeding hearts who didn't care about how the city's money was spent. All they seemed to want was to raise their expense accounts. But you can't run a city that way. And through it all, Rob was doing what he was really good at: keeping his eye on the finances, finding the efficiencies and holding everybody accountable, which made a lot of people go against him.

Things got heated a lot, and Rob got really quite outspoken at times. I never liked that, so I'd phone him as soon as he got out of council and give him heck for it. But at the same time, his brother would be saying, "Go for it! Don't let them get away with it!" That was definitely their father's influence at work, no matter how I felt about it. I sometimes thought maybe Doug Jr should've stuck with business instead of becoming a councillor. All those fights weren't good for either of them. I know Rob was lonely a lot of the time. He was married and had children, but he was away from home so much. I worried about him. How couldn't I?

RENATA FORD

I knew he had aspirations to become mayor. I thought, "Okay, maybe someday it'll happen," but it ended up happening a lot sooner than I expected. Our children were still very young when he decided to run, so I was hesitant. I thought he could still stay on as a councillor for a while longer. But he thought 2010 was his best opportunity, so once he'd made the decision, I supported him all the way.

On election night, I didn't quite believe it would happen. I knew he'd served his constituents very well, but I didn't realize how his way of just being genuine and speaking the truth had resonated across the whole city. People believed in him. It was incredible. When the votes were counted and he was named as mayor, I was too surprised and proud for words.

The kids really loved it. As Rob started to do the work of being mayor, the kids got the experience of watching their dad help people and serve the city. It was a good way for them to learn that hard work really does pay off.

I believed he was already the best mayor the city had ever had, but I also knew he would have to deal with the media and criticism and being in the public eye at all times. I did go down to see him at work a few times, but I really tried to avoid the attention and the media. Rob was the person who'd been elected—not me—and even though we talked about everything at home, my opinion wasn't necessary in public. Rob was the one who people wanted to see.

CHAPTER 14

Last Stop: Gravy Train

With the new mayor and council elected, there was a transition period of about two months, which meant we wouldn't fully "take over" until January 2011. Rob appointed Case Ootes to lead the transition team. Ootes, who'd been born in the Netherlands, was a steady, dependable guy. He'd served as deputy mayor under Mel Lastman, and after Lastman's mayoralty ended in 2003, Ootes stayed on as the councillor for Ward 29, Toronto-Danforth, until 2010, when he decided he wouldn't run for another term. The transition team had about 10 or 12 people under Ootes and was going to help us make the move from Miller's outgoing administration to Rob's new administration.

Nonetheless, Rob and I both went down to city hall the day after the election. The first thing we did was meet with

Cam Weldon and Joe Pennachetti, who were the CFO and city manager respectively. They both knew Rob from his time as a councillor, but they didn't know me at all.

"Look," said Cam, "we've got bad news. We're facing $774 million of pressure coming into this year's budget. We're going to have to raise taxes 25 percent to make up for it."

I think Rob expected something like this, but I was shocked. "How can things get to this shape?" I asked.

Rob and I both knew we were going to have to raise taxes or find efficiencies. Almost right away, Rob went for the efficiencies instead of raising taxes. "I'm going to find 10 percent right across the board," he said.

Neither Cam nor Joe looked happy. I later found out, after that first meeting, Cam told Joe he was going to quit, because he just wouldn't be able to deal with Rob's plan. He didn't quit, though; in fact, Cam and Joe both ended up staying on and doing a great job in helping us find those efficiencies.

ROB FORD

UPON BEING SWORN IN AS MAYOR OF TORONTO, DECEMBER 7, 2010

This is an exciting day, ladies and gentlemen. Many of us here in this chamber have been looking forward to this day for a long, long time. It's a day that we accept new responsibilities and begin new roles. It's a day full of hope and anticipation. It's also a day I'd like to say thank you. I'd like to take this opportunity to thank the people of Toronto for putting their faith in me. It is an enormous honour and privilege to serve this city as your mayor.

I'd like to congratulate each and every one of the 44 councillors here today. You each engaged with your communities and won their confidence in a long, difficult campaign. Victory on October 25 marked the end of those campaigns, and now the real work is beginning.

To new members who are joining us for the first time on council, I'd like to say welcome. I can say from personal experience, being a councillor for 10 years on the job, your beginning is one of the most difficult, but yet it's one of the most rewarding jobs you'll ever have. You'll have an opportunity that few people would ever enjoy. It's an opportunity to engage the people in your communities, to answer their calls, to understand their challenges, to walk in their shoes and to help them succeed.

When people ask me why I return every call, the answer is simple: it's respect and it's good customer service. I learned that from my father and my mother, who is with us today. Unfortunately, my father is not with us, but he is with us up above.

The truth is that it feels great to help people. I get to share in their lives in a tiny way. That's an amazing privilege. I encourage you to enjoy it. When you help someone out, the feeling is tremendous.

To the returning members of council, I'd like to say welcome back. Things are the same, but much has changed and more will change.

To the people of Toronto, who came out on election day in record numbers, I'd like to say thank you. You were engaged in this election on a level we haven't seen in generations. You spoke with a clear, strong voice. Every major candidate in the mayor's race ran on a platform of change. No matter who you cast your ballot for, you voted for change. That's a sobering reality for those of us on council to remember.

It's worth taking a moment to think about that, to put it in perspective, to understand where we as elected officials fit into the equation. Today, we are united in celebration. But in the days to come, this chamber will be the forum of many heated debates. Every time that happens, I believe it's important to remember one thing: the debate is not about us, it's about the taxpayers. It's important to remember that this council is not supreme, that the taxpayers are supreme.

As leaders of Toronto, we do not draw our power from the court. We do not draw our authority from the Crown. A higher level of government did not appoint us. We were elected by the taxpayers. The people are the source of our power, and the taxpayers of this great city are supreme. Whenever we are in doubt, we should remember that. The people spoke loudly and clearly. They're fed up with government leaders who feel entitled. They can no longer afford annual tax increases. They can no longer tolerate wasteful spending. They want that to stop, and that is what this council will deliver.

We have listened to the taxpayers, and our government will focus its agenda on four core priorities. Our first priority is customer service excellence. We will build a strong culture of customer service across every city department and agency. Customer service will be number one. All it takes is leadership, and leadership starts at the top, right here in this chamber.

Our second priority is to make government more transparent and accountable to the taxpayers, to the people, to the businesses. Hundreds of thousands of people engaged in our political process during this past election. They want a transparent government that is accountable, ladies and gentlemen. They want government to be effective and efficient.

Our third priority is to reduce the size and cost of government. Toronto taxpayers expect wasteful spending and annual tax increases to stop.

Our fourth priority is to create a transportation city plan. Transportation is not just transit. We will expand our focus that will include people that use transit, and also motorists, commercial vehicle operators, cyclists and pedestrians.

Delivering on these four priorities will meet the expectations of the people of this great city. It's an ambitious agenda and we will depend on this council for leadership. As members of city council, we must lead by example. We must understand that every dollar we spend, whether it's on firefighting, police services, is a dollar earned by a taxpayer.

People work hard for their wages. As their government, we must work harder. There is no bottomless pit of money. Every time we charge a tax, every resident must give up something we need or want in order to pay our taxes. To lead by example, we must be willing to give up some of our perks, privileges and the nice-to-haves.

For years, we've asked taxpayers to give us more, three percent here, three percent there. Now it's our turn to give more. We will reduce our spending at council and across all city departments. It is only fair and just. It is time city hall shared the burden we impose on taxpayers.

In closing, I'd like to add that Toronto's first mayor, William Lyon Mackenzie, was a bit of a rebel. He was a colourful character who was not accepted by the establishment because he fought against privilege and for the little guy. My plan is to be more successful than he was.

Today, we have a strong team of councillors committed to moving forward and working hard and doing what's right for the taxpayer. I encourage each and every one of you, whether you're elected to office, a leader in our community or you're just a passionate resident of Toronto, to join us in this cause. After all, we are all in this together, ladies and gentlemen, and together, we will succeed to make Toronto the best place to live, work and play. Thank you very much.

As the transition period went on, the time came for the committee chairs to be appointed. Our long-time friend Doug Holyday was given the position of deputy mayor. Paul Ainslie was given government management, Cesar Palacio was made chair of licensing and standards, and Denzil Minnan-Wong took public works. Michael Thompson was made chair of economic development. Mike Del Grande was appointed budget chief, as Rob had already decided back in the summer, and I was given the budget vice-chair position. That was fine by me—I didn't want a chair position. We needed to hand the chair positions to other councillors in order to bring them onto our side, and there were only so many to go around. In general, the appointments were pretty effective, but giving Karen Stintz the TTC was an absolute disaster.

I was the only one to speak up against it. I said, "I don't know her and I don't trust her."

The next day, Nick Kouvalis approached Stintz and told her what I'd said. Stintz, in turn, wasted no time in coming back to me and asking whether what Kouvalis had told her was true. "You don't trust me?" she said.

I looked her right in the eye and said, "No, I don't. I don't know you at all, and I don't feel like you're the right fit for transit."

She blinked at me as if she couldn't believe what I was saying, and replied, "But we're going to build subways."

I shrugged. The decision had been made, and on the surface, it looked like Karen Stintz was on our side.

Sure enough, as things turned out, Stintz showed her true colours a year later when she switched from subways to LRTs and tried to resurrect Transit City.[1] In my opinion, Stintz's change of heart was a betrayal of Rob but a good way for her to gain favour with the left. She wanted to be mayor one day—she went so far as to register in 2014—and maybe she thought promoting LRTs was a good way to kick-start her campaign. In any case, Karen Stintz was our first, biggest mistake at city hall.

Otherwise, the transition was pretty good, and there was even a moment or two of good humour. For instance, there's a tradition at Toronto City Hall in which the outgoing mayor leaves a little note or gift for the new guy; David Miller left gravy packets hidden all around the office, because of Rob's promise to stop the gravy train. We got a pretty good laugh out of that.

One thing I will say about David Miller: he was honest. He was not into scams or backroom deals or deliberate misuse of taxpayers' money. He just got caught up in the bureaucracy. I believe it was his own so-called team at city hall that undermined him and got in his way.

As far as the budget went, we had to not only find the $774 million while maintaining a zero percent tax increase, but we also had to do two budgets in one year in order to get the city's finances straightened out. Part of achieving this meant doing something that had never been done before: going through the budget line item by line item to identify the savings and efficiencies. This was a painstaking process that took all year, pretty much day in and day out. I give Mike Del Grande credit for being the budget chief, because that guy worked his butt off through the whole process.

We ran the two budgets—for 2011 and 2012—through as quickly as we could, because there really wasn't any time to mess around. In a four-year term, you only really have the first three years to realize your agenda; after that, you have to start focusing on a re-election strategy. The budget for 2011, in particular, had to come into effect on January 1. In any case, through our line-by-line analysis, we managed to find a surplus of $150 million, which helped us to stick to our zero percent tax increase. At the same time, we got rid of the vehicle registration tax.

Those budgets were a major early victory for Rob. Another victory—also an early one—was getting the TTC designated as an essential service. This had been one of Rob's campaign pledges, and it prohibited the right to strike by the TTC's unionized workers. The provincial government had to give it their blessing as well, which they did, with only a handful of NDP MPPs voting against it.[2]

At the same time, we did come up against a TTC fare increase in 2011. Rob was dead-set against it and held out for as long as he could, but in the end, he had to relent on a 10-cent increase.[3] Karen Stintz advocated pretty hard for the increase, which maybe should've seemed to us to be a sign about her loyalty. On the whole, however, we were happy with the outlook for transit at the time. Through our line-by-line analysis, we'd even found $16 million to offset other costs and problems.

Meanwhile, there were thousands and thousands of people on the city payroll, spread out everywhere, filling up the unions. But much of it was duplication. There would be a supervisor or manager who would report to another manager, who would report to another manager, and none of them would really have any workers underneath them, so the result was 10 tiers of middle managers reporting to a supervisor, who reported to someone else, and none of them were really doing anything except justifying their own jobs. The entire city staff was bloated—like many other levels of government. In some ways, I think Miller's administration had hired all these people as a result of pressure from the unions, but at the same time, I know civil services always feel like they need more people. More and more people—especially middle management—is not the answer. The answer is running things more efficiently and maintaining more accountability. It's as easy as that.

That was the mentality we brought to city hall. I know it put a lot of people on edge, on high alert, for a while, but it was a much-needed change in the mindset. Through this whole process, we were very fortunate to have Doug Holyday on our side, because he was an instrumental negotiator in these new labour contracts. It was a good balance, actually, since Doug had the ability to negotiate those contracts while Rob had the backbone to stand up to the union leadership and make sure that both the front-line workers and the taxpayers were protected. By the middle of 2011, we'd offered buyouts to staff.

As far as obvious efficiencies went, the decision to privatize garbage collection was a no-brainer. We did a study that compared garbage pickup in Toronto with that in Hamilton, where a private company was doing much of it. In an area of similar size, the Toronto guys were picking up 600 loads a day, whereas in Hamilton it was 900 loads. We found that in our system, the operators often wouldn't gas up their trucks until the morning. Whereas with the private garbage collectors, the trucks would be filled up the night before and be ready for the drivers first thing in the morning. In Toronto, the drivers would come back to the yard to have their lunch. In Hamilton, the drivers didn't come back to the yard for lunch, because that would be an hour or more out of their routes, which cost them money. In Toronto, the trucks in the fleet were smaller, so they had to be emptied more often. The private outfit had invested in larger trucks, so they wouldn't have to be emptied so often. These all seem like little things, maybe, but they were exactly the kind of efficiencies we were looking for.

So after a council vote of 70 percent in favour, we contracted the pickup services west of Yonge Street to a company called Green For Life, and within a little under two years, the city had saved almost $12 million.[4] On top of that, Green For Life was a lot better at responding to customer complaints than the unionized garbage crews working everywhere else in the city. Despite the differences we had with him later on, Denzil Minnan-Wong was a major player in putting the privatized collection plan together, and I know he got a lot of heat from the lefties on council.

As of this writing, Toronto hasn't extended the privatized pickup from west of Yonge to the rest of the city, mainly thanks to renewed pressure from the unions and their friends on council.

Then there was city transit—a topic that still drives up my blood pressure whenever I have to talk about it. For starters, neither Ontario Premier Dalton McGuinty nor Miller could get any stimulus money from the federal government, because the Transit City plan didn't meet the quick timelines the feds had laid out for their investment.[5] The next piece of the puzzle was the province pulling their commitment to the funding. So that delayed a bunch of the planned LRT work. Then there was the St. Clair Avenue streetcar right-of-way project, which came in at over $100 million dollars (against an initial projection of $48 million); and St. Clair *still* needs refitting work to this day.[6] And, surprise surprise, much of the work being done was sole source—another practice that drove Rob crazy.[7] On the whole, Transit City was an absolute disaster.

Rob always believed that the reliance on LRTs and other forms of surface transport—at the expense of subways—meant that Toronto basically had a two-tier transit system. The subway lines (as they presently look) and some streetcar routes work well for everyone in midtown and downtown, but everyone in the suburbs and north of the highway has long been screwed over. Having to rely on bus routes just doesn't cut it for the folks in the suburbs. (On that note, Rob used to say that if everyone in Etobicoke, Scarborough and North York would come together and vote as a block, they wouldn't be ignored by the downtown elites, and they would be strong enough to have all the subways they'd ever need.)

From the outset of his mayoralty, Rob knew that transit was always going to be a fight, but I don't think he knew how much of a fight. Part of it, in my opinion, was personal. There were councillors who would vote against Rob no matter what issue was on the table.

At the same time, while we were trying to figure all of

this out, Rob firmly believed in protecting the front-line people. It wasn't their fault that there was so much mismanagement above them. At the management level, there were layers and layers of inefficiencies.

Not only did we find $774 million, I believe we were the only government at any level to actually spend less money one year than we did the year before. It stunned Prime Minister Stephen Harper. When we met him, he asked Rob, "How did you spend less money one year than you did the previous year?"

The answer was that people knew not to screw around with Rob when it came to the budget. He was direct and simple about wanting to get things done. He wouldn't tolerate any dicking around. But the challenge for us, as in any government, is that you have to get everything done in the first few years. So from 2010 to 2013, we just pushed our agenda through as hard as we could. We balanced the budget the first year, with a zero percent tax increase. That's critical to know. We spent less money one year than we did the year previous, and the taxpayers had a zero percent tax increase.

One major way Rob managed to balance the city budget was with a 10 percent reduction in everyone's operating budgets. He simply said, "We want 10 percent reduction." From there, we helped the bureaucrats figure out ways they could achieve those reductions. Then they came back with their proposals. Most of the city services met the targets in their proposals or came fairly close.

It was harder to get a few services to play ball, however. The most prominent of these was the Toronto Police Service. Chief Bill Blair gave Rob serious resistance on the 10 percent target, right from the get-go. In my opinion, that's where the tension started between them.

As with all other front-line workers, Rob loved the police. But he saw the chief as a problem. Not only did Blair not want to make the 10 percent cut, he actually asked for an almost 2 percent increase.[8] Looking back, maybe we should have brought in a new chief who was more of an ally. In any case, Blair worked out a plan to make his 10 percent cuts over two years, which was a lot longer than any other department was allowed.

Rob was a powerhouse, and he was willing to do what it took to get the job done. Even when I disagreed with decisions Rob made, a lot of the time all I had to do was wait two or three weeks, maybe a month, before Rob would inevitably be proven right. He did love to say, "Jones, I told you so."

The thing is—and even to my surprise—Rob just had the pulse of the people and generally knew what was going on well before the newspapers or the professional pollsters knew. It all came back to that same old customer service model: calling people back. Rob was talking to upwards of 80 people a day, sometimes more, from every background and every part of the city; he listened to them and heard what they were worried about. I don't know how he tracked all the information, but he did. So when it came to talking to people and understanding the political landscape, he was his own walking pollster.

THINGS WERE GOOD as we made our way through the first year of Rob's term. Things were very good. Our successes, I felt, were unparalleled. That's not to say there weren't roadblocks and obstacles and even some strategic mistakes. Appointing Karen Stintz as the chair of the TTC was our first misstep; the second mistake was appointing Nick Kouvalis as Rob's chief of staff after the election. I had had a bad feeling about the appointment—I'd always found Kouvalis to have a bit of a "Nick first" attitude.

On the other hand, Kouvalis had been with us through the whole campaign. Loyalty was hugely important to Rob and me. We'd always wanted to take care of and help out the people who'd done right by us along the way. On top of that, Kouvalis told us he only wanted to stay in the position for a year or so, just to get things going, and then he'd move along. We took him at his word and gave him the job.

Anyway, it didn't last long. In February 2011, Kouvalis left, claiming that he wanted to spend more time with his family back in Windsor. (Within the year he'd moved on to help the federal Conservative Party with their campaign.)

In any case, after Kouvalis was gone, the chief of staff job went to Amir Remtulla, a public affairs expert from Molson Coors Canada. We had Remtulla until the summer of 2012, when he left to take a gig with the upcoming Pan Am Games. Remtulla was a great asset and a hard worker, and, as with Adrienne Batra, we were sad to see him go—although we fully understood how great an opportunity it was for him to move to Pan Am. With Remtulla gone, Rob appointed Mark Towhey as chief of staff. I had my reservations about this. For that matter, so did Rob. Towhey didn't seem to have much of a personality; he had a way of staying in his office with his door closed, and he did not see eye to eye with a lot of the councillors. That being said, he was smart and he had a good understanding of policy. Those were two major facets of his appeal.

There was also the question of loyalty. Rob had appointed Towhey from his so-called inner circle, which prompted a lot of criticism from Rob's usual opponents. But Towhey had been around since the beginning of Rob's run for mayor, and that meant a great deal. Rob felt as if Towhey had earned his position. He was next in line, in other words, and if Rob had brought in someone new over top of Towhey, then that would've been disloyal.

Well, Mark Towhey would definitely show his true colours, and his own brand of loyalty, when the time came, but I'll get to that.

Outside of these personnel issues, we also had the media circling like vultures, waiting for anything to make into a controversy. They'd tried to do this during the campaign, and it just hadn't worked, but now that Rob was mayor, there was no way the media were going to back off. At least in the beginning they had to dig pretty deep to find anything. The first convenient target the media had was labelling Rob a "homophobe" over the fact that he didn't attend the city's annual Pride parade. The truth was Rob didn't give a damn if someone was gay, straight, purple or pink. He would help whomever he could.

The leadership and organizers of the Pride parade didn't help. They seemed to have a way of trying to bully public figures into attending, also using the homophobe accusation for anyone they couldn't get to co-operate. (Never mind the other LGBT events Rob attended later in his term as mayor, and the proclamation against homophobia he signed and read in public in 2012.) For our whole lives, we'd always had a family gathering up at the cottage on the same July weekend when Pride activities would start. Rob had a choice: either go to the family gathering or go down to the parade. He always chose the cottage.

Rob also had a tendency to dig in his heels, for better or worse, whenever he felt someone was pressuring him on an issue. "No one's going to force me," he would say. I admired him for that, even if it drove me crazy as well. I told him to just skip the cottage weekend and go to the parade, but once Rob felt he was being pressured—as he did as soon as the parade organizers and media and some other councillors started mouthing off about it—he would not give in.

Despite how Rob handled the Pride parade, he never missed the Caribbean Carnival (a.k.a. Caribana) grand parade each summer. He was a huge advocate of Toronto's widespread and diverse Caribbean community, and he always praised the millions of dollars the carnival brought into the city's economy each year. The media, of course, was a lot less interested in covering Rob's participation in this particular festival. His absence from the Pride parade seemed to be the whole story. Funny how that works.

I remember Rob getting "in trouble" when he was spotted talking on his cellphone while driving along the Gardiner Expressway. Some lady was in the car in the next lane, taking pictures of him while he was talking. It made the *Toronto Star*, but as with many other things, Rob just came out and said, "Yeah, I was on the phone. I'm a busy guy." Giorgio Mammoliti defended him on this one; Mammoliti said Rob was a hard-working mayor who didn't have anyone chauffeuring him around but was still making time to return calls.[9]

Now, as much as I think the media were just digging for dirt with the driving-on-the-phone story, I also thought Rob should've had a driver. He was entitled to one, but of course he didn't want to take advantage of that entitlement because it was a public cost. On that note, I also thought he should have had a police security detail as well. Here, in fact, was another story the media tried to get some mileage out of. To summarize: Rob made the decision to close the interior doors to the mayor's office (David Miller had always left the interior doors open) and not publish his meeting schedule. The schedule would be available after the fact, by requests made to Adrienne Batra. The *Star* published an article called "What Does Rob Ford Do All Day?" which seemed to imply that Rob was hard to track down and meet with, as if to further imply he wasn't doing his job.[10]

The truth behind the closed doors and the unpublished meeting schedule was that Rob, unlike David Miller, was getting constant threats. By the middle of 2011, two men had already been arrested and charged in two separate incidents.[11] Rob tried to downplay it all, but it was pretty scary. The threats didn't stop with Rob, either. There were threats made against his wife, our mother, me, my wife and my daughters. There were, and still are, a lot of bottom feeders and sick people out there who, for whatever reason, developed a special hatred for us—I guess because of our political views and what we were trying to do to fix the city. Anyway, the media wanted to depict Rob as being evasive in not sharing his schedule, but in truth, it was about security and taking precautions—as well as about his constituents' privacy, since the media would follow Rob on constituent calls. It's funny because, as far as I know, John Tory doesn't give out his schedule and hasn't reopened the interior doors of the mayor's office, but the media doesn't seem to be interested in that story.

Then there was the time when CBC's *This Hour Has 22 Minutes* pulled a prank on Rob at his house early in the morning one day in October 2011. Mary Walsh, as her Marg Delahunty character (wearing red armour and carrying a sword), tried to more or less surprise Rob into an interview. At the time, Rob was just coming out the front door with his daughter, Stephanie, to take her to school before he continued on to his office at city hall. Stephanie was frightened and Rob was confused and the whole thing turned into a bit of a fiasco. The *Star*, among a bunch of other media outlets, seized on it as a way to take a swipe at Rob: here was the mayor calling 9-1-1 when it was just a 60-year-old lady with a plastic sword in his driveway.[12]

But of course the media didn't tell Rob's side of the

story. Rob never watched *This Hour Has 22 Minutes* and had no idea who Mary Walsh or her character was. All he knew in the moment was that there appeared to be some nutcase with a sword in his driveway, first thing in the morning, and how much it upset his daughter. This was coming at a time when our family had received multiple death threats, as well. So I think it was pretty understandable that Rob didn't exactly play ball in that situation. Sadly, I guess I wasn't surprised at how the media tried to spin it, either.

CHAPTER 15

Selling Toronto to the World

To be sure, even with the media circling and other challenges, there were some great moments for us. For example, in 2012, Prince Charles and Camilla came to Toronto, as part of their royal tour of Canada, to see a Victoria Day fireworks show down at Ashbridges Bay. A number of first responders were invited, as were Premier Dalton McGuinty and his wife, Terri. Rob and Renata were also invited, but Renata was unavailable, so I went as my brother's plus-one. A park on the bay had been designated for seating for the event; the area had been cordoned off and lawn chairs had been set up. The plan was for Prince Charles and Camilla to arrive by boat, escorted by the RCMP. As we were waiting in the seating area, Rob and I were given protocol instructions by some of the staff. We were to call the prince "Your Highness" when we first met him. After that, we could call him "sir."

Anyway, just as the sun went down, the boat with the prince and Camilla arrived. There was a quick meet-and-greet, and then all the handlers and staff got down to business, showing everyone to their seats. The seating was arranged like a horseshoe; the idea was that the head seat would go to Prince Charles, with Dalton McGuinty on one side of him and Rob on the other. Camilla, Terri McGuinty and I (in Renata's place) would all sit together on another side of the horseshoe. But it seemed as if the British handlers weren't sure which Ford brother was which, because before I knew it, I was seated beside Prince Charles, and Rob had been consigned to my seat between Terri McGuinty and Camilla, 20 feet away. By that point, the show was about to start and there wasn't anything anyone could do about it.

I wasn't sure if Prince Charles was able to tell us apart either, but then as the fireworks started, he said, "Doug, who's paying for this show?"

I had to laugh. I pointed at McGuinty and said, "Your Highness, the guy beside you is on the hook for the fireworks, because Rob and I sure aren't paying for them!"

That got a laugh from the prince and even from Dalton McGuinty himself.

I looked over at Rob. He was trying to make small talk

with Camilla and Terri McGuinty. But he caught me looking at him, and he glared at me. I knew that look. It was Rob's way of saying, *You're dead, Jones.* All I could do was grin back at him. Later on, even Rob had to admit how funny the whole mix-up had been.

Then, in September 2012, Rob and I put together a trip to Chicago to see if we could rekindle business relationships, meet their mayor and generally promote Toronto. We brought 80 people—mostly businesspeople but also a handful of councillors and city staff—with us, and everyone paid their own way. None of it was expensed to the taxpayers, including Rob's and my expenses. We had Bob Deluce, CEO of Porter Airlines, as one of the co-chairs and our friend George Cohon, the founder of McDonald's Canada. George had a number of business friends in Chicago, including the owner of the White Sox, Jerry Reinsdorf. That was especially great, because we were able to go to a White Sox game and take a guided tour of their field and offices.

Then we met with the mayor of Chicago, Rahm Emanuel, who'd previously served as President Obama's chief of staff. I'll never forget the meeting. When Mayor Emanuel pulled up to the hotel to meet us, you'd have thought some head of state was in town. There were three black SUVs and all kinds of security personnel. Rob and I shared a laugh about it, because Toronto's bigger than

Chicago and Rob never had any kind of entourage like that. It was a good meeting for Rob and Emanuel. They renewed the 1991 Sister Cities agreement and talked about a bunch of areas in which the two cities could learn from each other—things like infrastructure, transit and city staff management.

Rob's meeting with Emanuel was a great opportunity, but my favourite part of the trip was an impromptu meeting with Illinois Governor Pat Quinn. He and Rob and I tossed the football around in his office—this was the kind of diplomacy I could really get behind!

Overall, Rob was extremely pleased with the trip. The whole thing culminated with a boat tour of Chicago's beautiful waterfront. The waterfront in the Windy City features parks and sports facilities and fancy restaurants and wildlife enclosures. The whole thing is a hugely successful tourist attraction and revenue generator. I'd spent years travelling to and from Chicago, so I knew all about the waterfront and had thought Toronto could have a similar attraction. I'd even come up with a plan for it back in 2011.

Right now, the Toronto Port Lands is a big parcel of property, 900 acres or so. Much of the land isn't developed in any cohesive fashion; there's even a garbage dump on the end of one of the piers. Waterfront Toronto has had some kind of redevelopment plan in the works, but hundreds of millions and several years later, there's been no movement on it. This is some of the most valuable property in Canada. As I saw it, we could have an excellent entertainment complex down there—something to rival or surpass the CN Tower and Toronto's handful of other sightseeing areas. Part of my plan included installing an observation wheel. The media wanted to depict it as if I was advocating for a Ferris wheel, like some kind of carnival attraction, but what I wanted was something similar to the London Eye, which has been a major commercial success for London. There are 24 other major cities with observation wheels, and we wanted to make it a tourist destination. In my plan, the rest of the Port Lands complex could feature museums, concert venues, animal sanctuaries, high-end shopping and hotels, and whatever else the market dictated. We wanted to raise billions of dollars in revenue by selling off the property.

I had Rob's support for the plan, but council quickly aligned themselves against us. Councillor Jaye Robinson, Ward 25, Don Valley West, led the charge to vote against us. Council wanted to stick to the city's original waterfront plan, no matter how long it would take and how much money would be spent for it to happen.

Voting our plan down was a mistake. We could have generated significant revenues through an accelerated development of the Port Lands, not to mention the tourist attractions that would have gone in quite quickly. On top of that, everything would have been paid for by the private sector.

The ironic thing about this came later, on that trip to Chicago. A few of those councillors who'd voted against my idea—Jaye Robinson, for one, as well as Michelle Berardinetti—saw Navy Pier when we were out on that boat tour, and they said, "Look at that pier. We should do that in Toronto."

On the one hand, I had to laugh. On the other hand, I also had to consider how many councillors hadn't had the opportunity to travel and see how other major cities worked, the way I had.

THE WATERFRONT AND CHICAGO trip notwithstanding, and not counting the media, Rob's biggest problem was council itself. From the beginning, there were a few councillors who openly aligned themselves against Rob, no matter what was to come. Adam Vaughan (Ward 20, Trinity-Spadina), Shelley Carroll (Ward 33, Don Valley East), Janet Davis (Ward 31, Beaches-East York) and Josh Matlow (Ward 22, St. Paul's) were probably the most prominent, and not surprisingly, all of the wards they represented were downtown or close to it. I wouldn't go so far as to call them "enemies," but they certainly made a habit of trying to stop Rob wherever they could or turning their backs on him in council sessions.

As a matter of fact, Josh Matlow had a radio show called *The City* that aired on Sunday afternoons on Newstalk 1010. He loved to get on there and chirp away at us for two hours. He and his guests would criticize Rob's initiatives, such as the Scarborough subway and the elimination of the land transfer tax, or he'd use the show to give a platform to second-rate media muckrakers like *Now Magazine.*[1]

So I finally called up 1010's program director, Mike Bendixen, and I said, "I'll make you a deal. We'll take over the show, Rob and I, and your ratings will go through the roof."

Sure enough, we took over *The City* from Matlow in February 2012 and the ratings immediately shot up. But more importantly—and it took us a little while to realize this—the show gave us a way to unofficially set the agenda every Sunday for the following week. We had every councillor, as well as a good number of politicians from beyond city hall, tuning in to hear what we had to say. So in that sense, we had Matlow to thank for the opportunity—even if he might not have agreed.

Apart from Matlow, Adam Vaughan was probably the worst of Rob's critics. He tried to get in Rob's way about everything, from Rob's football coaching to his bullshit conflict-of-interest trial to his tough-on-crime ideas.[2]

Having some left-wing ideas is one thing, but I think these councillors were obsessed with protecting union leadership and spending public money. It seemed to me that none of them had any comprehension of balancing the books. I could only shake my head in disbelief—we were trusting these people to be leaders?

Then, later in 2012, another ridiculous obstacle presented itself. This was a conflict-of-interest case, brought against Rob by a private citizen, and it was something between an annoying distraction and pure horseshit. The whole thing started back in 2010, right in the middle of our first campaign. To summarize: Back when he was a councillor, Rob had raised $40,000 for his football foundation. He'd used his office letterhead to reach out to various corporations to help him with the fundraising. After some complaints about it from other councillors, the integrity commissioner, Janet Leiper, ordered Rob to refund the donors a little over $3,000, which Rob had used as start-up costs and spent on football equipment. In turn, Rob asked why Leiper wasn't investigating "the $12,000 retirement party for Kyle Rae or the $6,000 French lessons for Adam Giambrone."

I personally thought those were damn good questions to ask. Besides, every councillor would send out letters for various fundraising efforts—although those generally seemed to be in support of the arts. (I think if Rob had sent out letters for an arts project or environmental issue, there never would've been a problem, but football didn't seem to fit into what the lefties considered important.) Anyway, Kyle Rae's retirement party and Adam Giambrone's French lessons didn't make it onto the commissioner's radar. Neither did a number of closed-door sole-source deals that Rob also pointed out. But for some reason, that $3,000 he'd raised for the foundation was of great interest to her.

Anyway, it went to a vote in late August. The lefties voted for the motion and won. Initially, Rob tried to give refunds, but he quickly found that his donors didn't want the money back; they'd long since filed their taxes with these charitable donations factored in. Plus, the legal basis of the whole thing was pretty shaky. Rob hadn't personally benefited from the donations, nor had he asked for money to go straight to him, so it was difficult to call it a conflict. So he challenged it, and for the time being, the whole stupid thing slipped to the back burner, and we were able to refocus on running the city.

As we moved into 2012, Rob wanted to finally put the whole football conflict to bed, so he asked council to vote on a motion whereby no further action would be taken, and the whole case would be closed. Well, the motion carried, and that was that . . . almost.

But then in March 2012, Paul Magder (not the Paul

Magder of Magder Furs fame) showed up on the scene and brought a lawsuit to the Ontario Superior Court, arguing that Rob had violated the Municipal Conflict of Interest Act. The reasoning was that Rob had spoken about and voted on the conflict thing in council, which put him in conflict again. This was over $3,000 that had been spent on purchasing football equipment for underprivileged young people. Rob didn't know this Magder guy and neither did I, but he seemed intent on going the distance with my brother like nothing I'd ever seen before. And he even got Clayton Ruby to represent him pro bono.

Anyway, it turned into a circus pretty fast. The trial took place in the fall, and initially, the judge ruled against Rob. It even looked as though Rob was about to lose his seat. But then we appealed, and by early 2013, the finding of the Superior Court was overturned. From there, Ruby tried to take it to the Supreme Court of Canada, but they rejected it. We were obviously pretty happy and relieved. It had been almost a year and a half of nonsense and time wastage. And fortunately for Mr. Magder, the court also ruled that he wouldn't have to pay the $116,000 in legal fees that Rob had racked up defending himself, but that's another story. At least the football conflict was finally over.

Not that problems with activists were over for Rob—or for me, for that matter. In 2014, another private citizen, a woman named Jude MacDonald (who'd sat outside Rob's office for a year, protesting his term as mayor), launched an application to the Superior Court that once again said there'd been some conflicts of interest. For starters, MacDonald said we (as in Deco, our family business) had done business with a prominent airline, and so every time Rob or I voted in favour of expanding Toronto's island airport, she said we were putting ourselves in a position to make financial gains.

At first, I had no recollection of doing business with the airline. So I looked into our files. Sure enough, before I was a councillor, this airline had put in some small orders for some decals. Deco was the only company that made decals with the required adhesive, so we got the business—but it was small and I was never directly aware of it.

MacDonald also said that Deco had done business with a large bottled water company. This was also a limited contract and it had happened many years before. In any case, the vending machines at Toronto City Hall didn't sell bottled water. You could get Coke and Pepsi and all the sugary drinks, but you couldn't get bottled water. During my time as a councillor, this ban on bottled water went to a vote, and I voted in favour of restocking the machines with water. That was enough for MacDonald and her friends to find a conflict of interest, because of the bottled water company Deco had done limited work with several years before. Anyway, MacDonald recently withdrew her application.

These conflict of interest cases were so aggravating because it showed us that there were people out there who just couldn't accept that the majority of the Toronto electorate had voted us in. There were people who would stop at nothing to bring us down, because they couldn't stand how we were disagreeing with them or their special interests or whatever else. I don't know why. I do know it was exhausting.

I found the conflict accusations upsetting because they implied that we could be bought. If a politician can be bought, it takes no time for the word to get out. No one could buy us. No special interest groups could influence us. No one even tried, because they knew we'd call the cops on them straightaway. Even when Rob was a new councillor, getting his feet wet, no one tried it, because he'd already started to make a name for himself as the guy who was hunting down the corruption and the scandals.

The problems in Montreal with politicians are well known; numerous public figures have lost their jobs over their ties to organized crime. I think we in Toronto have wanted to believe we don't have the same problems here. We do, although in our case, organized crime is not the issue. In our case, it's political donors who think that a

$1,000 donation to a campaign should get them favours, like transferring land agreements or changing zoning from industrial to residential or whatever else it is that they want.

And does it? You seldom see this kind of thing end up in front of the integrity commissioner or the court. But even if it's legal, if it happens, it's wrong.

In any case, Rob thought all this business with the integrity commissioner was little more than an aggravation. It just rolled off his shoulders because he knew he was innocent. He knew it was a witch hunt. It was more of a distraction to me than Rob. I would try to handle all the bullshit that came his way, whereas he mostly said, "Ah, who cares. I never did anything wrong. Ignore it, Jones."

I did my best to take his advice as much as I could, but that didn't mean we didn't spend a fortune on lawyers. On the home front, our wives and kids hated the politics and the attacks in the media. My daughter Kara did a broadcast television course at Conestoga College, and one day her class went on a field trip. While they were having a tour, their guide badmouthed Rob the whole way, not knowing who my daughter was. Karla complained to the teacher, who apologized, but the damage of it—the stress for Kara, the feelings of persecution and helplessness—was already done. And that was really just a drop in the bucket. Having said that, we've always been fighters, my daughters included, and nobody ever once thought we should give up.

Outside of city hall, our family stuck by us through thick and thin. The workload was demanding. It felt like I was never home; I was always at events, always running from one place to the next—and I know Rob was even busier. My daughters were in high school at the time, and Rob's two kids were in elementary school, and it was very hard to be away from them. Politics is a lot to ask of a family. On top of that, the harassment and threats made it all the worse. It's one thing to have someone threaten to fight you—Rob and I had had plenty of scraps playing hockey over the years—but nowadays, it seems that instead of someone throwing a punch, they're more apt to shoot you. In that case, it doesn't matter how tough you are. I always wondered what we'd done to make certain people hate us so much and, I guess, see us as less than human.

I will admit that the job took an emotional toll on me—far more than I expected it would. I'd say it took its toll on Rob too, but he had thicker skin than I did. He knew the game, and he'd always tell me, "Doug, never say it's a thankless job, because it's not."

And he was right. Whenever we were away from city hall—whenever we were out in public—the sentiment was usually non-stop thanks from the people on the street. People would tell us to keep going, don't give up. They were behind us all the way. Even today, I'll walk out and hear the same comments from people I've never even met before. That's what gave us the energy. The media and the establishment and the elites were saying one thing about us, but the public—the silent majority, as we called it—were saying something else.

CHAPTER 16

The Silent Majority

My first couple of years as a councillor were more of a learning curve than I'd ever imagined. I wanted to take the business approach that had always served me well at Deco. I found out it wasn't as easy as that. For starters, if a councillor wants to make a change of some kind, he or she needs the vote of the council. That means a lot of ass-kissing. You might think you have a few colleagues on your side, but most of them will drop off pretty quickly if it suits them. My dad knew that, Rob knew that, and before long I knew it too—I had to be very careful about who I trusted.

Luckily, everything in Ward 2, Etobicoke North, was in good shape. I honestly felt like I had the best ward around. Rob had built such a strong reputation there by answering his constituents' calls and showing up at their doors. All I had to do was take that good old customer service model and carry on. And if I didn't, if I slipped behind once in a while, Rob would call me up and let me have it. He'd tell me to get my ass over to Mrs. Smith's house, or to fix the crack on some side street, or to help someone with their garbage collection. He still knew everything that was going on in the ward, because a lot of folks still called him. It was good, though. It kept me focused.

I will admit how exhausting it was, working as a city councillor. Going into the role, I'd anticipated some of this exhaustion, but I hadn't really understood what I was in for until I was doing it. The job was 24/7. I was lucky to have such a great team in my office to help me out, but I was still astonished by the amount of work that needed to be done (maybe that's the amount of work that needs to be done when you're dedicated to doing the job right). Anyway, I'd wake up quite early most mornings, generally around 6:00 a.m. I had to be out of the house and heading to city hall no later than eight, and the whole way there, I'd have to fight the streetcars and the bicycles.

Toronto traffic was another thing that took me by surprise, because prior to my term as a councillor, I'd never needed to go downtown very often. So I couldn't understand why Rob would get so ticked off with the cyclists and the streetcars. But then it was my turn to drive along Dundas Street or Queen Street during the morning rush hour. I'd have the streetcars creeping along one lane and the bicycles taking up the other lane, and I'd just be stuck behind them. I found some of the bike riders especially dangerous. They'd cut me off or ride right through red lights. There was something careless and reckless about them. In the suburbs, it's much different; people use their bikes to ride on the trails or the side streets or other calmer areas. But many of those downtown riders were a menace.

Then there were the streetcars. I remember bringing some guys from Chicago to visit Toronto, and when they saw the streetcars, they asked me if we were living in the early 1900s, because the streetcars seemed so antiquated. I can't count the number of times I got stuck behind a streetcar that was stalled because its antenna had come off the overhead cable. I'd watch the driver hop out and run around to the back and use a long pole to try to hook the antenna back up, all while there were a hundred cars clogging up the street behind him. The answer is subways, subways, subways. It would take me an hour, sometimes more, to get from my home in Etobicoke to city hall. It often felt as if I could get to Pearson airport, catch a flight to Chicago, land and clear customs in less time than my commute as a councillor.

During my commute, I'd always listen to radio talk shows. I preferred AM640, but it was always instructive to listen to Newstalk 1010 to hear what the angry lefties were saying about us. That, at least, would give me some forewarning about what the day ahead was going to bring. Quite often, by the time the lefties had finished their call-in rants, our own communications people would be calling me in the car to prepare me for the same issue. They'd warn me about whatever had happened the night before or what surprise item was on the agenda for the day. Or they would tell me that some media scrum was already in the parking lot, waiting for me to get to city hall. I could barely even get out of my vehicle before the media would be in my face, almost from day one. Conniving, ruthless, relentless.

Having said that, on the whole, we felt as if the first two years of Rob's mayoralty were hugely successful. We got a ton of stuff done and we saved the city over a billion dollars, while keeping the lowest tax rate for any major urban centre in North America. Every developer knew the city was open for business under Rob's administration. At one time, we had more cranes working in Toronto than in New York, Chicago, LA, Dallas and Boston combined. We were very proud of what we'd accomplished.

Even with our successes, I wasn't planning to run again as a city councillor as we looked toward 2014. I was considering a run as an Ontario MPP, because there would be a provincial election in 2014, and I'd already had enough of city politics. Rob was definitely thinking of a second term as mayor, though. And he would've been unbeatable. Even John Tory said to me, "I would've never run [in 2014] because I couldn't have beaten him." So that was the plan.

But then things got really complicated.

CHAPTER 17

Under Fire

I was using cocaine, I was using marijuana. All these new designer drugs I'm not into, but I was snorting a lot of cocaine and smoking a lot of dope. It all started from drinking, though. I would be drinking and by the time I killed a two-sixer, I'd be going on a 40, and that's when all the coke comes, and everything else comes after the alcohol. The alcohol is the devil. It's the worst drug around, bar none. It leads you down to paths that some people never come back. I'm surprised some nights I've survived.[1]

—Rob Ford, in an interview on AM640's *Bill Carroll Show*, October 1, 2015

On Thursday, May 16, 2013, the *Toronto Star* ran the now infamous story.

Rob Ford in 'crack cocaine' video scandal

A video that appears to show Toronto's mayor smoking crack is being shopped around by a group of Somali men involved in the drug trade.[2]

It was huge front-page news, and in no time at all, it had gone viral across the country. The American website Gawker also ran the story, which was picked up throughout the US and overseas.

As soon as I could get Rob alone, I said, "Is this true?"

"No," he said, point-blank.

I didn't know what to think, but hearing the word "no" from his lips, I believed him. I had to believe him. It was only the beginning of the craziness that would follow.

By 2013, I'd become aware of the drinking and partying rumours about Rob that were starting to make the rounds. These had started as early as the year before. The most well known of the rumours was that Rob had had a few too many and stayed out way too late on St. Patrick's Day of 2012. Of course that made the papers and the news. Politicians and public figures are constantly being watched and videoed with phones, but it's easy to forget this. Even Rob could forget about the scrutiny from the public, because he usually had a thousand other things pressing on his mind. At first, the St. Patrick's Day incident didn't really bother me. I always believed I could trust Rob with a few beers or a shot of Scotch underneath his belt more than any other "straight-laced" politician in the country, and even after a hard night out, Rob would deal with the issues and return the phone calls.

There was also another, far more personal aspect to Rob's drinking: I never saw him do it. He kept me completely in the dark about it. I remember going on AM640 once and saying that unless you have an alcoholic in your family, you don't really understand how it works. They can either be out in the open about their alcoholism (or drug issues), or they can be in the closet about it. I believe Rob was a closet alcoholic, at least when it came to his family. Whenever I was with him, he didn't drink at all. But I usually wasn't with him after work hours. When the workday ended, I'd go home to Karla and my daughters. Rob would go home too—but then he sometimes went back out later in the evening. I just wasn't privy to this side of him.

In the interview Rob gave shortly before he died with AM640's Bill Carroll, he said, "Doug didn't know how bad my disease was. You think he was out covering up for me, but even my other brother, my sister and my mom, they didn't know. It was how bad I was. You know what? I was running around thinking everything was okay, and meanwhile I was just fooling myself, but more importantly, I was just making a complete fool out of myself, and I wasn't pulling the wool over anyone's eyes."[3]

Rob and I shared so much that it might seem hard to understand why he kept me in the dark about his drinking. I never cared too much about someone smoking a joint, even if I didn't myself, but when it came to the hard stuff—heroin, cocaine, pills, uppers, downers and whatever else—I always stayed far away from it. I'd seen how much damage it could do, and on top of that, I never liked the idea of losing control of myself in a situation. To that end, in my opinion, alcohol isn't much safer, even if it's legal. To this day, even in my own house, I don't drink. I keep booze there for when friends visit, but I don't partake myself. I just don't trust it.

All this is to say, I'd always thought that Rob largely shared my beliefs. I knew he didn't take the same hard line about drinking that I did—he definitely liked to have a beer or two—but for the most part, at family functions or any time he was around me, he didn't drink at all. Later, when the extent of his problems started to become clearer, I heard from some of his buddies that his policy, more or less, was "Don't tell Doug." He knew I was apt to tear a strip off him if I'd known how hard he was drinking.

I even asked him, after the St. Patrick's Day stuff, if he was going a bit too hard. He said, "No, no, no. I don't know what you're talking about." In retrospect, that was his defence mechanism going up.

For a long time, I took him at his word. We were crazy busy with city hall issues at the time anyway, and it felt like we didn't have time to focus on this stuff. That may seem short-sighted, but I also thought this was yet another thing the media had dug up and blown way out of proportion. They'd gone after Rob for just about every other thing they could—usually to no lasting avail—so here was an opportunity to accuse him of being a drunk. Never mind how many stories there were of other mayors and councillors who liked to have more than their share of drinks while in office; this was Rob Ford.

On the other hand, back in 2010, when the media had run the story about the Florida joint incident, it actually helped Rob's campaign, because he admitted to it and it humanized him. The same thing happened, with some communities at least, with his drinking in public. For example, I remember speaking to some visitors from Poland who'd been down on the Danforth; they'd seen Rob eating a hamburger and drinking a beer and hanging out with a whole bunch of people. They said, "That's the mayor, and he's out in public eating a hamburger and having a beer with a whole bunch of people?" These Polish people couldn't believe it, but they also loved it, they told me. They'd never seen that kind of thing back home.

So in a way, Rob was *real.* That was part of his appeal. The trouble was, he became a little too real. I just wish I'd known sooner.

OUTSIDE OF THE DRINKING rumours, we were happy with our accomplishments at the end of the first two years of Rob's mayoralty. We'd done more for the city in those two years than the previous administration had in seven. But subways were still the biggest bone of contention, and a major stressor. The fact is, subways make sense. Virtually every major city in the world has a subway system. They build those systems one kilometre at a time and just keep them going. They never take their tunnelling machines out of the ground. But Toronto has had a hard time getting it together.

We had a great plan. After Transit City had been scrapped, we pushed hard for a three-stop Scarborough subway extension, all the way up to McCowan Road. This came with a promise of a little over $1 billion from the provincial government, as well as $660 million from the feds. In other words, we managed to get all three levels of government to play ball—something that Transit City was not able to achieve.

With the funding in place, we managed to get council to vote in favour of the plan. Paul Ainslie was the only Scarborough councillor who voted against it. Of course, all the downtown councillors, more or less led by Josh Matlow, voted against it as well, once again showing their disinterest in a workable transit system for the suburbs and the neighbourhoods north of the 401. It was there. The plan was in place, ready to go . . .

I say this with a lot of frustration, because as of this writing, three years later, Toronto transit is still completely off the rails, so to speak. John Tory has reduced the Scarborough subway to one stop along the route, costing an estimated $3 billion, God knows why. Meanwhile, the ridiculous LRT plan has been resurrected by the usual suspects, like Josh Matlow (who, ironically, has six subway stations in his ward). And stuck in the middle of this fight are the residents of the suburbs, who still can't get around their city in an efficient way. This, to me, is the exact kind of thing that summarizes the dysfunction of Toronto city council.

Not that subways were going to be the only fight we faced outside of the drinking rumours. By early 2013, with the media watching Rob's every move, other people started to see an opportunity to pounce and drag him down. One of them was Sarah Thomson, a magazine publisher who'd failed in a bid for the mayoralty back in 2010. After she'd dropped out of the race, she'd thrown her support to George Smitherman.

Anyway, the Canadian Jewish Political Affairs Committee held an event on a Thursday evening in March. Rob was there, as were a number of other public figures. At one in the morning or so, Thomson found the most unflattering picture of Rob she could, with her standing next to him, and posted it online. Then she tweeted that Rob had asked her to come to Florida with him and grabbed her ass.

I was furious when I heard it, because I was sure it was complete bullshit. It just wasn't something Rob would do. Because of his weight issues, he was very insecure and shy, especially around women. He was not a womanizer whatsoever. Now, if someone had told me they were in a bar and saw Rob get in a brawl with another guy, I'd have been a lot more inclined to believe that was possible (depending on the circumstances leading up to the brawl). But groping a woman was out of the question.

In some ways, it looked as if it was going to be Rob's word against Thomson's, but fortunately for us Greg Beros, a city councillor from Richmond Hill, came forward to say he overheard Thomson describing to her assistant the whole thing—the awkward photo and the alleged groping—before it happened. According to Beros, Thomson even said it would be good for her campaign (she ran for election again in 2014).[4] If this whole initial incident with Rob wasn't enough already, Thomson also showed up at our Scarborough Ford Fest in 2014—on horseback.

Initially, Rob wanted to sue, but he knew that would have become a whole story on its own, so he was happy to just let it go. It was a troubling sign, though. Imagine a hockey game where you have one player in particular who's a rising star but also has a reputation as a scrapper. For sure, someone from the other team wants to be a tough guy, so he thinks to himself, "Okay, I'll go up and give this rising star a go." He does, and he gets his ass kicked for it. But it doesn't end there, because there's the next would-be tough guy waiting to take a shot, and then the next one after that. And maybe these guys have better sense than to pick a one-on-one fight with the rising star, so they go for the cheap shots, or two or three of them try to pile on at once. That's what I saw starting to happen with Rob and the Sarah Thomsons of the world.

Looking back, as frustrated as I was about subways and people like Sarah Thomson, they were nothing compared to how the shit hit the fan after the *Star* ran its crack scandal story on May 13.

CHAPTER 18

Roller Coaster Ride

The day after the crack story ran, Rob gave a quick statement to the media: "These allegations are ridiculous," he said, before pointing out how many other times the *Star* had gone after him for bullshit reasons.[1] For my part, I was still in shock; to this day, I don't even have the words to describe how I felt. But, as I said before, I believed Rob. And it *did* seem like bullshit.

For one thing, there was the photograph, now pretty infamous, of Rob standing in an Etobicoke driveway with three young men who were supposedly connected to the drug trade. One of the young men in the picture, Anthony Smith, had been shot and killed in some kind of fracas a couple of months before the crack story came out. The photograph is worth talking about because it was treated as "proof," at least as far as the media were concerned, of

Rob's connections to the underworld, but in fact it was one more small aspect of the whole story getting blown way out of proportion. I say this because Rob was one of the most photographed politicians in the country, if not the world. For the time Rob was in office, tens of thousands of pictures were taken of him at events and with people of all stripes. He'd never walk away from taking a picture with someone if they asked.

So this picture of Rob and Anthony Smith and the other guys was really just another picture. It so happened that these guys had criminal backgrounds, but I guarantee there were scores of other people with records in pictures with Rob. When a member of the public says, "Can I take a picture?" you don't ask to see their ID or their passport or if they have a criminal record. But, I suppose, you also don't expect the media to be working overtime, like ravenous dogs, to find connections and scandals wherever they possibly can. And they were even worse as soon as the crack allegations came out.

There was talk about a video floating around in the Dixon Road high-rises somewhere, but at that time—May—there was nothing substantiated. Robyn Doolittle and Kevin Donovan from the *Toronto Star* had said they'd seen *something*, but what? And US-based Gawker, well-known as the kind of media outlet that publishes celebrity sex tapes and gossip, was raising money—again, for what exactly? I was concerned and confused, to be sure, but given how unsubstantiated everything seemed, it's understandable how firmly I took my brother at his word.

Consider what Rob himself had to say about the video, a long time later: "I still haven't seen the video. I still want the whole world to see it, and then I can maybe explain it, but I can't explain something that I have yet to see. I understand the media have seen it, I understand everyone else has seen it . . . I don't even remember some of the nights. I don't know how I got home sometimes. I didn't get home some nights. I woke up on park benches some mornings . . . I hear through the grapevine that I wasn't even coherent in this video, but I haven't seen the video, so if the video comes out, I'll be more than happy to come on the air and try to explain what it is."[2]

Either way, we didn't have a media strategy at first. The plan was just to offer no comment and move the conversation along. For starters, it was hard to figure out an exact message on something like that, so we wanted to stay focused on the daily items and the running of the city. Those issues weren't going away; it was still constantly busy.

Still, despite our best intentions, the media were everywhere. *Everywhere.* I'd thought they were bad before—I had no idea how much worse they could get. The weekend directly after the crack story had run was the Victoria Day long weekend. That had always been a major get-together time for us at the family cottage, but all of a sudden, we had journalists from different outlets stalking the property. They were in the bushes, trying to get pictures of us. My daughters, who had nothing to do with any of it, were too uncomfortable to go outside and enjoy the weather. It was infuriating.

I was sufficiently pissed off that I decided to give some remarks of my own to the press when we got back to work a day or two later. A little conference was easy enough to set up—the media had been hounding me for comments as much as they'd been hounding Rob, as if they thought I was his spokesman. In many ways, I was his spokesman, but I was also his brother, and that's how I approached it.

I'll admit it felt good to have a chance to strike back at the media. "He is the people's mayor," I said. "Never has the mayor been so accessible or cared so much for the big issues facing residents. His attention to the needs of constituents is what has made Rob Ford mayor of Toronto. Now our mayor faces yet another accusation, an accusation driven by reporting from a news outlet that has proven they would do anything to stop the mayor's agenda. Rob is telling me these stories are untrue, that these accusations are ridiculous, and I believe him."[3]

I reminded them how Rob had dedicated most of his life to serving the public. I pointed out Rob's fiscal leadership, labour deal negotiations, budget balancing and other accomplishments. I talked about how our family had been unfairly pulled into the mix. I talked about the way the media were denigrating Toronto's Somali community, which was frankly racist. I didn't pull any punches in my comments, and I made it clear that we wouldn't be doing anything except on our own terms and timelines.

But the drama that day didn't end with my tearing a strip off the media. May 22 was the same day that Don Bosco told Rob he wasn't allowed to coach football anymore. The school administration claimed the dismissal had nothing to do with the crack video, but without question, in my mind, it was a political manoeuvre. A lot of kids went to Don Bosco because of the football program Rob had started. But he'd made enemies at the administrative level.

Back in March, Rob had given a "man cave" interview to David "Menzoid" Menzies on Sun News; in that interview, Rob talked about how he'd started the Don Bosco team with his money back in 2002. He also talked about the rough lives some of his players had come from—gangs and broken homes and that kind of thing—and how he made them stay in school in order to play football. As long as those players graduated from high school, Rob said, even if they never played football again, he was still "the happiest man on two feet" for them.[4]

These might have seemed like inspiring and heartfelt comments, but for some in the school administration and on the parent council, it was enough to get rid of him. The co-chair of the parent council, Teresa Bridport, spoke to the *Toronto Star* (surprise surprise) and said Rob didn't know how to speak and that the school would be better off without him, even while admitting his "heart [was] in the right place" and that she and the other parents "appreciate[d] the time he put in for the football program."[5] That was that—Rob was let go.

It was hard for me to believe the trouble at Don Bosco wasn't another opportunistic attack on my brother. In any case, it couldn't have come at a worse time, given the other issues that were underway. Looking back now, I think Rob's dismissal from Don Bosco was actually a much, much bigger problem than even he realized, but this is a point I'll return to later.

Loyalty was very important to Rob. Case in point: Rob's chief of staff, Mark Towhey. I had had my reservations about giving Towhey the role in the first place, but Rob had wanted to recognize him for how long he'd been on the team and how hard he'd worked during the campaign in 2010. But ultimately it didn't work out the way Rob had hoped and Towhey was fired on May 23, 2013.

Rob phoning a potential constituent during the first campaign he won, in 2000, when he ran for city councillor in Ward 2, Etobicoke North. He had run in 1997 and fallen short, but he'd learned a lot of valuable lessons on the trail. Rob always made a point of returning as many phone calls as he possibly could, even as late as midnight if need be.

The Fords during the 2000 election campaign.

Michael Ford with Rob. Many years later, after Rob passed away in 2016, Michael would win a by-election in Ward 2 with almost 70 percent of the vote, becoming the youngest Toronto councillor in recent memory.

Election night in Ward 2, in 2000. As usual, I was by Rob's side, and our dad, the political veteran, supported us in everything we did.

A quiet moment for Rob, our dad and me at our home on Weston Wood, 2002. Doug Sr was an incredible businessman, politician and father. He died too young, at 73 years of age, in 2006.

Rob with my daughters Krista (*left*) and Kara at an early Ford Fest, 2003, supporting the city's firefighters. We love and support all emergency responders.

Rob and Renata with Stephanie, 2004.

The city park beside our home on Weston Wood was renamed in Dad's honour as Douglas B. Ford Park in 2010. Rob, Randy, our mom, Kathy and I are so proud that our dad's name graces such a beautiful part of the city.

Rob celebrating a victory as a coach with the Don Bosco Catholic Secondary School's Eagles. Rob spent endless hours working with the youth of the city, particularly those from disadvantaged homes. He was often criticized for the time he spent coaching at Don Bosco, when really he should have been celebrated for giving back to the community. (Photo by Christopher Drost/Canadian Press)

Rob with family friend and former federal finance minister Jim Flaherty at Ford Fest, 2006. Jim supported us through thick and thin, and his emotional response to Rob's challenges in the media demonstrated how much he cared about our family. Sadly, Jim died suddenly on April 10, 2014, and the country lost one of its finest leaders.

With our mom, Diane, and Frances Nunziata, city councillor and speaker of Toronto city council in the summer of 2010.

Rob and Renata's son, Dougie, during the Toronto mayoral race in 2010. I was so honoured when Rob told me he was naming his son after our dad and me.

Two brothers, one vision. The night Rob was announced as the winner of the mayoralty race, the family rejoiced at our home on Weston Wood. Ten years of hard work paid off in a big way. (Tyler Anderson, *National Post*)

When Rob was elected mayor of Toronto on October 25, 2010, the taxpayers finally had a voice at city hall. Although he'd rarely led in the polls leading up to election night, he triumphed in the only poll that mattered: he won the election, getting almost 100,000 more votes than the runner-up, George Smitherman. Rob immediately set to work as the people's mayor, cutting taxes and putting a stop to the gravy train at city hall. (Tyler Anderson, *National Post*)

Rob asked the inimitable Don Cherry to swear him in at Toronto City Hall on December 7, 2010. Grapes, who never shies away from controversy, took some heat for calling out "left-wing kooks" and for saying that the suit he was wearing was "for all the pinkos out there that ride bicycles and everything." Randy (*left*) and I were so happy to see Rob rightfully take over the mayor's seat and to finally bring accountability to council.

Rob and me lining up in the mayor's office, January 20, 2011. Rob and I were huge football fans and hoped to bring an NFL team to the city. I had stepped away from my role at Deco to take over Rob's seat in Ward 2 and continue the family tradition in politics. (Alex Urosevic/*Toronto Sun*)

Mayor Rob Ford in his office, surrounded by family photos. (Photo by Peter Power/*The Globe and Mail*)

Rob and I were honoured to host Governor General David Johnston and his esteemed wife, Sharon, in 2012.

Rob and his family after he was voted in as mayor in 2010. Renata, Stephanie and Dougie were Rob's heart and soul.

A few days later, Rob would lose George Christopoulos and Isaac Ransom, press secretary and deputy press secretary, from his staff. These were surprise resignations at the time, as far as I knew, but I saw it as a failure to stick it out when things got tough. Ransom later said that Rob had been with a woman who might have been an escort on his St. Patrick's Day drinking binge.[6] The "escort" turned out to be Alana Kindree, Miss Toronto Tourism 2010.

I personally think it is a big problem to assume someone is an escort just because she's a young, attractive woman out for a few drinks. Furthermore, in Rob's capacities as councillor and mayor, he had met countless people—like Kindree—who enjoyed hanging around with him because of his approachable, regular-guy appeal.

Over the next week or so, three more of Rob's staff left—Brian Johnston, Kia Nejatian and Michael Prempeh. The story in the media depicted these as resignations, but after Towhey left, and the sudden departures of Christopoulos and Ransom, and the inside information starting to leak out in dribs and drabs, Rob knew he finally had to make some tough decisions, even if it meant being short-handed. But these were hard times, and loyalty could no longer be questioned in any way.

Earl Provost took over from Mark Towhey in May 2013 and stayed on until November of the same year. Earl had also worked on Rob's campaign in 2010 and was one of many strong Liberals who worked in Rob's office over the years. I am still in contact with Earl today.

Dan Jacobs was Rob's last chief of staff; Rob and I both believed Dan was the best of the bunch. Outside of city hall, Dan was (and still is) a close friend of our family's. He was always there for us, right through Rob's battle with cancer, until the very end. These days, Dan works as my nephew Michael's executive assistant.

MAY GAVE WAY to the summer of 2013. One of Rob's newest critics was Ontario Premier Kathleen Wynne, who in the wake of the crack allegations threatened to intervene in the city's administration if needed.[7] Any criticism of Rob coming from Wynne was pretty rich—here she was helming a government that had under her predecessor wasted billions of dollars of taxpayers' money over the gas plant fiasco, the eHealth boondoggle and the Ornge air-ambulance disaster, among other scandals. In fact, her government was facing a confidence vote that was poised to bring them down. In my opinion, the blatant mismanagement at the provincial level was a disaster. And here she was yapping off like a parrot about my brother. I find it ironic that even during Rob's worst times, his polling numbers were double what Wynne's are today.

Even more troubling than Wynne's comments was the

growing tension with the Toronto Police Service's leadership, specifically Chief Bill Blair. Throughout the summer, the police conducted a bunch of raids as part of their Project Traveller operation. Numerous drug dealers were arrested and hundreds of guns were seized. However, during all of this, some anonymous police sources "leaked" information to the media that Rob's name had somehow come up in connection with the raids. Now, there was nothing specific about this supposed link, and as the *National Post* observed: "It's also worth noting that merely being mentioned, or the alleged video being mentioned, in a wiretapped conversation doesn't constitute evidence of wrongdoing against Mr. Ford."[8] But nonetheless, this little tidbit of leaked information was enough to send the media into a renewed frenzy of speculation and accusation, which actually seemed to overshadow what Project Traveller was really about.

Officially, Chief Blair stayed noncommittal about the leak throughout the summer, but it sure was convenient for him. For one thing, Blair had been the only one to give us massive grief, back in 2011, when we asked each city department to cut 10 percent from its budget. For another thing, Blair was in a spotlight of his own over a couple of different controversies. There were plenty of ongoing lawsuits and inquiries about Blair's leadership during the G20 in 2010, especially about who at the police command level had ordered mass arrests downtown.[9] Blair's name frequently came up during these inquiries. Blair also had the police shooting of 18-year-old Sammy Yatim—caught on video—to deal with.[10] Despite the tensions with Blair, Rob and I always stood behind the front-line police 100 percent; our support for them never wavered. We differentiated between those front-line officers and a chief who wasn't on the same page as Rob.

Finally, Chief Blair had also become quite close with Andy Pringle, who was a member of the Toronto Police Services Board. Pringle had taken Blair on a fishing trip to New Brunswick in 2012. Pringle actually paid for the trip, which raised some serious concerns about a potential conflict of interest.[11] Pringle had also served as John Tory's chief of staff when Tory was an MPP. Rob expressed some concerns to me: he believed Pringle and Blair were interested in having John Tory take over the mayoralty in 2014, since Tory was of the same kind of politically friendly establishment as Blair himself. We were disappointed in Pringle.

None of the above could absolve Rob of his demons—demons I had yet to fully understand—but he and I both firmly believed he was a convenient political scapegoat for high-profile figures like Kathleen Wynne and Bill Blair when they were dealing with their own issues.

But throughout it all, we were sticking to business as usual as much as we could. The downtown lefties were all running around, pulling their hair out, making noise about Rob resigning, which he was in no way prepared to do. In fact, according to the polls, Rob was still widely supported for re-election in Etobicoke, Scarborough and North York. As Rob himself said, the only poll that truly counted was election day 2014.[12] To that end, we were intent on Rob running again (personally, I'd decided that one term as a city councillor was enough for me—I was thinking of maybe running at the provincial level, or maybe just returning to Deco). And why wouldn't we want Rob to run again? Financially, the city had never been in better shape, and even while Rob's enemies in the media and politics were attacking more viciously than ever, Ford Nation had never been more supportive. In a way, Rob running for re-election was a counterattack, and it felt like the right thing to do.

Fortunately, we weren't alone. We had countless supporters in the public, many of whom were sick and tired of the media feeding frenzy in particular. A number of private complaints were made to the Ontario Press Council, mostly about the sensationalist way the *Toronto Star* had reported the story about a crack video nobody had seen (and nobody presently knew the whereabouts of).

In September, a series of public hearings was held at Ryerson University. Darylle Donley was the woman complaining against the *Star.* She had concerns about the fairness of the way they'd reported the crack story.[13] Complaining against *The Globe* was Connie Harrison, who said the extensive use of anonymous sources made it impossible for her to know what or who to believe.[14] The editors-in-chief of both papers were called up on the carpet to account for their reporting.

The complaints were all dismissed. That wasn't a big surprise, to be honest—the council had no lawful power in the first place, and beyond that, it was stacked with media cronies anyway. But we saw it as an embarrassment for the *Star* and *The Globe*, and it finally gave a platform to some regular folks—like Donley and Harrison and everyone else who'd made a complaint—to have their voices heard.

NOTHING GOT EASIER as we moved into the fall of 2013, but our focus on business as usual and Rob's re-election campaign was yielding a lot of positive results. The *Toronto Sun*, at least, lauded Rob's accomplishments, in spite of the scandals that were dogging us, calling Rob a "refreshing change from the indifference and arrogance Canadians often encounter at all levels of government"[15] and calling attention to his accomplishments on behalf of taxpayers. Rob also conducted a highly publicized touring blitz of some high-rise apartment buildings under the administration of the Toronto Community Housing Corporation.

He'd toured the same locations as a councillor 10 years earlier and was now generally pleased to see improvements to the residences, although there was still work to do. In true Ford customer service form, he made sure every tenant received a business card with his home phone number on it, so that he could keep a personal eye on the repairs he was promising.[16]

Toronto was also preparing for (or being prepared for, depending on how you look at it) the 2015 Pan Am Games. Toronto's selection as the host city had happened back in 2009, under David Miller's watch. Not surprisingly, during the planning process, a culture of entitlement and runaway expenses had risen up around the Games' top officials—$2,000 car rentals, $8,500 for a hotel room and cocktail party, countless claims for coffee, tea and parking tickets, and bonuses to six-figure salaries—all on the taxpayers' dime.[17] The provincial government, under Kathleen Wynne, seemed fairly uninterested in doing anything about the out-of-control spending. So Rob had a meeting with the Games' chair, David Peterson. After Rob threatened to boycott the Pan Am Games, Peterson finally agreed to conduct better oversight of the Games' expense policies.[18]

There were some good times, too. That August, Rob participated in the Great Ontario Salmon Derby, along with his counterpart Hazel McCallion, long-time mayor of Mississauga. At one point, McCallion, then 91 years old, had a tug on her line hard enough to almost pull her overboard. Rob caught her in a bear hug, in full view of many cameras. It was a rare moment of lightheartedness and humour in an otherwise difficult time. A month later, Rob was able to take a delegation down to Austin, Texas, to meet with then-mayor Lee Leffingwell and learn about his city's thriving culture, especially its vibrant live music events. With events as big as Austin City Limits and South by Southwest, thousands of jobs are created in Austin every year. This was something Rob wanted to emulate with Toronto's own music and arts scene.

Last but not least, there was the re-election to focus on. In June, I made it official that I wasn't going to run but that I would be by Rob's side. Election mode was where Rob was in his top fighting form. Other 2014 mayoral contenders included John Tory (certainly not to our surprise, as we knew the establishment had been lining things up to have him take another run at it) and Olivia Chow, the heavily left-wing former city councillor and wife of the late Jack Layton. Rob had minimal worries about campaigning against either of them. But then, in late October, Karen Stintz also announced her candidacy. As I've said before, appointing Stintz as head of the TTC was the biggest mistake we'd made; she'd flip-flopped and backtracked and proved my reservations right. Now she was saying she wanted to have a go at the top job. This was a challenge

Rob was very happy to take on; in his own words on our radio show, he was "absolutely salivating" at the chance.[19]

That was how things stood for us as September turned to October. We were fighting hard, hitting back at our enemies every chance we got. Despite all the ups and downs, I'd never been so proud to be by my brother's side.

ON THE MORNING of November 5, 2013, I held a press conference at city hall. I spoke strictly as myself and not on behalf of Rob or council. I made it crystal clear that I had unwavering support (as did Rob) for Toronto's front-line police officers. Then I went on to call out Chief Blair for what I saw as his posture as judge, jury and executioner and for what I was sure was his clear political bias against my brother.

A few days earlier, Blair had held a press conference of his own. He'd talked about some computer files that had been seized as part of Project Traveller, including the alleged video of Rob smoking crack. Blair had gone on to say "I'm disappointed" about whatever it was he'd seen in those files.[20] For me, this was the tipping point. Enough was enough. The problem was this: I didn't know what was on that video. Nobody knew, except for the people who claimed to have seen it. What I did know was that my brother had not so far been charged with any crime whatsoever, yet what

I heard sounded like the city's top cop essentially calling Rob guilty—at least in the media's kangaroo court.

I wasn't the only person to feel this way. Senator Bob Runciman, who'd served as Ontario's solicitor-general (and who therefore might be considered an expert on these things), had come out with some comments of his own about Blair's press conference. "I can't recall anything like his [press] conference and his unnecessary comments . . . the video and his disappointment," Runciman said, and added, "If police resources were used for political purposes, that should alarm everyone, including Ford haters."[21] The former premier of British Columbia, Ujjal Dosanjh, summed it up even more tersely, by tweeting that Blair should "Charge, put up or shut up. That's the rule for non-political police."[22]

The chief's unnecessary comments about Rob were troubling enough on their own, but there was also Sandro Lisi to consider. Lisi had been charged with extortion in connection with the case. To this day, I don't know how Rob got introduced to Sandro Lisi. I believe Lisi came on the scene when all the controversies were really reaching their peak, but I wouldn't have known him if he'd walked past me, which I'm sure he did many times. Lisi was part of that other side of Rob, the side he kept secret from me. But whoever he was, Lisi deserved a fair trial—same as anybody else charged under the Canadian criminal justice system.

(Fortunately, as of this writing, summer 2016, Sandro Lisi has had all charges against him dropped.)

So after Blair held his press conference, I went on the offensive. I called Blair out for what he'd said, and I called him out for the fishing trip he'd taken with Andy Pringle. If Blair was going to get political, I thought it was more than fair for us to get political in response. What was Blair's agenda? What plans did he have for my brother and for his own career? In my conference, I plainly stated that Bill Blair and Andy Pringle should both step down, and I asked the Police Services Board to launch a probe. Some of the reporters at the conference asked if I was ready to start a "war" with the police chief.[23] I replied by saying I wasn't intimidated by him, and I wasn't. To me, it was a matter of fairness.

Before I wrapped the press conference up, some reporters asked me why Rob wasn't there. I told them Rob was out answering calls, as he did almost every other day. And as far as I knew, he was doing that. I had no idea that Rob was going to hold an impromptu press conference of his own that afternoon.

CHAPTER 19

Late-Breaking News

I had business to conduct away from city hall for the rest of the morning. I can't remember what it was, but I know I was gone until the late morning. I remember that because I was pulling back into the parking lot when my other brother, Randy, called me.

When I answered the phone, Randy said, "Did you hear what's on the news?"

"No," I said. "What?"

Randy took a moment before replying. "Rob just came out and said he smoked crack."

Sure enough, as I turned on the radio, it was all over the news. From what I could gather, Rob had just stepped out of his office, into the usual throng of reporters, and laid it bare: "Yes, I have smoked crack cocaine . . . Probably in one of my drunken stupors, probably approximately about a year ago . . . Yes, I've made mistakes. All I can do now is apologize and move on."[1] Then he'd just turned around and gone back into his office.

For a little while, I just sat in the car. I was stunned. I couldn't believe what I'd just heard. A few hours earlier, I'd gone hard, maybe a little too hard, after Chief Blair for the way I thought that he'd been demonizing Rob. A lot of what I'd said may have been fair game, but at the same time, I'd spoken my mind in the firm belief that Rob had told me the truth, that the video was a hoax, that he'd never smoked crack. I'd had no idea he was going to make this admission.

Now . . . Well . . . Now what?

After I gathered my bearings, I went inside and straight up to Rob's office. There were reporters everywhere, but I managed to get inside the office without too many problems. I found him sitting at his desk. He didn't seem surprised that I was there, but he also couldn't look at me. In fact, he wasn't looking at anything in particular.

After a moment of silence, the only thing I could think to say was, "You weren't honest with me, Jones. I asked you straight if any of it was true and you looked me in the eye and said no. We can deal with anything, but that? What am I supposed to think?"

When he finally responded, his tone of voice was quiet—almost relieved. "I needed to get this off my shoulders," he said. "I've got nothing else to hide. I've come clean with everyone. I told them what I did." He went on to say he'd been worrying about the video, which he'd still never seen, and how it might be released. Rob didn't know what was on the video, but he knew for sure he didn't want to be a hostage to it, whatever it was.

I sat down on the other side of his desk. "Do you need help?" I said.

"No," said Rob. "It was a one-time thing. I smoked it in a drunken stupor, but that's it. I'm not an addict."

As things would turn out, crack really wasn't the issue, but even Rob had yet to understand the problem.

NEEDLESS TO SAY, things turned into even more of a madhouse after Rob came clean about smoking crack. There were physical altercations between some of the journalists crowding the halls outside of Rob's office, all of them vying for the best spot to get their microphones into his face as soon as he would appear. The American media were circling too, and Rob's problems began making the rounds on all the late-night shows—*The Daily Show* with Jon Stewart, *The Late Show with Stephen Colbert*, *Jimmy Kimmel Live*, even *Saturday Night Live*. We had former pro wrestler The Iron Sheik show up at city hall unannounced, as part of some kind of media stunt, to challenge Rob to an arm wrestle. Apparently, this was meant to be an intervention. (Rob had beaten Hulk Hogan in an arm wrestle a few months before.)

The mysterious crack video *still* hadn't shown up. By this point, even Rob called for it to be released to the public; he wanted to see what was on it as much as anyone else did, and respond to it. But another video appeared, this one sold by an anonymous source to the *Toronto Star* for $5,000.[2] In this short video, Rob was animated and possibly drunk. He was sounding off about someone—we never found out who. When he went off on a tangent like that, his bark was a lot worse than his bite, and anyway, many people say things behind closed doors that they don't intend for a wider audience. Rob obviously hadn't intended for this conversation, whatever it was, to be caught on video. Rob was embarrassed by this video's release and offered yet another public apology.

That same day, our mother and our sister, Kathy, did an interview with CP24's Stephen LeDrew. It was an emotional half-hour interview for them. Our mother said she was heartbroken about the whole thing. Kathy mentioned how hot under the collar I'd become, jumping in to defend Rob at every turn, which was true. But both Kathy and our mother agreed that Rob had been relentlessly attacked by the media, to the point that all the good he'd done for the city had been totally obscured.

Our mother talked about how Rob's kids couldn't even go out to play in their yard anymore, because Rob's house was besieged by reporters.[3]

Our mother and Kathy were right: the impact on our family *had* been devastating. This wasn't lost on Rob at all, as he later said in his interview with Bill Carroll, "As you know . . . every family has their challenges. Every family has personal problems. Every single one. Some are more severe than others, some are more exposed than others, and in our case, the whole world saw what was happening to myself and my family. The last, last people I want to hurt are my mom, and my brothers and my sister, my beautiful wife and my kids, and my late father upstairs. It was . . . Sorry . . . I'm just getting . . . It's tough. It's tough but it's done. The damage is done and I can't change the past, but I know one thing: I'm sure as hell going to change the future."[4]

Well, the opportunity for Rob to change the future was still a little while away. In the meantime, we just needed to survive the craziness. By the end of the week, following a meeting with Newstalk 1010's Mike Bendixen, we learned our radio show was ending. It had been a good run, but we knew, going forward, we wouldn't be able to focus on any topic other than Rob's problems, and there was already enough of that all over the TV, radio and newspapers.

Apart from the media circus, city council was also starting to tighten its circle around Rob. Back on November 5, when Rob had made his unannounced admission about smoking crack, I believe he'd hoped his honesty and humility would resonate with the rest of the city leadership. Unfortunately, it had the opposite effect. At best, Rob's honesty brought out a lot of holier-than-thou finger-pointing; at worst, the opportunists were seeing their chance to go in for the kill.

It began with a bunch of councillors putting forward a motion for Rob to take a leave of absence. This was led by Denzil Minnan-Wong, who'd long been one of our allies. All the usual suspects—Adam Vaughan, Josh Matlow and Jaye Robinson—voted for it (Karen Stintz, amazingly, was absent from the vote), but we were sorely disappointed to see the likes of Mike Del Grande and Frances Nunziata voting for the motion as well.[5] I could only interpret it as a misguided sense of care for Rob. The motion passed, but since it didn't carry any official weight (council can't make the mayor step down or take a leave of absence), it was little more than a high-profile stunt. Since drug use was a theme in the motion, Rob responded by launching a motion of his own, namely having every member of council drug-tested by December 1. This motion was unsuccessful.

During these debates, things got pretty heated. It seemed Minnan-Wong had positioned himself as the ring-leader, and at one point, he and Rob got face to face on the council chamber floor. The confrontation had the same feel as some of those old industrial league hockey games, so I went over to take Rob by the arm and cool him down before Minnan-Wong pushed him too far. We all took a short recess after that.

In any case, with everything that was happening, Rob just couldn't catch a break. He was being attacked on all fronts, and even now, it amazes me that he kept it together as well as he did. His opponents on council were still making noise about removing him from office, but since they couldn't do that, they voted to strip him of his powers instead. At that point, Rob still hadn't been criminally charged with a single thing. The successful way he'd run the city hadn't changed, so it was hard not to believe the pile-on was anything other than personal or political.

The pile-on wasn't limited to city council. It wasn't limited to the provincial level, either. After Rob had his powers stripped, one more high-profile person came out of the woodwork to take an opportunistic cheap shot at him: federal Conservative Jason Kenney, minister of employment and social development. Outside of the House of Commons, Kenney said Rob should "step aside and stop dragging . . . Toronto through this terrible embarrassment."[6]

Sadly, then–prime minister Stephen Harper didn't have much to say in Rob's defence, but Jim Flaherty did. He publicly stood up and said Rob was "still my friend."[7] It was such an honest, simple thing to say. Rob was so incredibly moved by the show of support and friendship that he was encouraged to keep fighting. Not six months later, Jim Flaherty passed away from a heart attack, leaving a major hole in Canadian politics.

CHAPTER 20

Infamy

November was coming to an end and Christmas was on the horizon. Although Rob was asked not to attend the Toronto Santa Claus Parade, he still made it out for a smaller parade along the Lakeshore in Etobicoke. Marching along the street with Santa Claus, handing out candy, was the exact kind of thing he loved doing, and it was a much-needed boost for his mental well-being at the same time. There were countless folks lining the sidewalks who were happy to see him, as well. When asked by a *Toronto Sun* reporter what her opinion was, one Etobicoke parade attendee said, "I would still vote for Mr. Ford, yes . . . He does a great job. That's all that matters. What he does in his personal life is his business."[1]

Around the same time, both of us sat down with CBC's Peter Mansbridge to talk about everything that had happened. This was an opportunity for Rob to speak plainly about city council's move to strip his powers: "The people elected me, the largest mandate in Canada's history, and they just stripped my powers," said Rob. "They gave me 25 percent of what David Miller had. I return thousands of calls. I can't function as the mayor of Toronto with eight people in my office. They just stripped me of everything I had because of [my] personal problems . . . Not one person brought up how much money I saved the taxpayers." Rob also added that he felt he was being punished for telling the truth and was getting kicked while he was down. "I let my mom down, I let my brothers down, I let my wife down, my kids down, and I let my dad down. I know he's upstairs watching us."[2] Most importantly, Rob made it clear that he intended to seek re-election in a year's time.

When Mansbridge asked me my opinion, I kept it simple: "Everyone needs a second chance," I said. "Rob's the champion of second chances."[3]

Looking back on it, in fact, I think the Mansbridge interview was the time we started to really push back and stand our ground against the pressure from the media and the political elite. For one thing, Rob did an interview with Conrad Black (another person who'd been pilloried by the establishment after paying his debt to society). During this conversation, Rob openly voiced his concerns about what he saw as Chief Blair's political agenda and using Sandro

Lisi as a stooge to get to Rob. "If I've done something illegal, I've told the police to arrest me," Rob told Black.[4]

Around this time, Rob and I also worked with the Sun News Network to launch a *Ford Nation* show. Unfortunately, this didn't work out; our show was too resource-intensive for the network to maintain. But it's interesting to note that our solo episode was the network's top-rated program of all time. After that, we took our show to YouTube.

Just before Christmas, a major ice storm hit the Greater Toronto Area. Hundreds of thousands of residents lost power in their homes, and streets all over the city were paralyzed with fallen branches and other debris. Despite the other things happening, Rob immediately stepped up to deal with the problem. Folks in low-income and subsidized housing were hit especially hard as the interiors of their homes froze. Rob toured these neighbourhoods endlessly, knocking on doors, reaching out to people, urging them to move to the various warming centres the city had set up. At the same time, Deputy Mayor Norm Kelly—who'd inherited most of Rob's powers when council had stripped him—was on vacation with his family in Florida, where he worked on the crisis from a distance.[5] As the city's services worked hard to get things back on track, Rob made the decision not to declare a state of emergency (one of the mayoral powers he still possessed). As he put it, "We don't need it . . . What a state of emergency could do is put people in a panic. And we don't want to panic people right now. Things are progressing very well."[6]

Rob's efforts were helped enormously by the president of Toronto Hydro, Anthony Haines, Toronto Fire Chief Jim Sales and city manager Joe Pennachetti, not to mention scores of city staffers. At the same time—as residents were still freezing in their homes—Premier Kathleen Wynne absolutely refused to have anything to do with Rob, choosing instead to communicate only with Norm Kelly. If that wasn't crazy enough, Wynne did not recall provincial Energy Minister Bob Chiarelli from visiting family in Ottawa to help Toronto Hydro deal with the problem. When criticized about this, Wynne simply said, "It's not about passing judgment on each other"—as though her refusal to interact with Rob was somehow not exactly that![7]

In any case, Rob's tireless work during the ice storm—with or without the support of the province—reflected well on him. A Forum Research poll conducted with the *Toronto Sun* showed Rob's approval had gone back up to 47 percent. Forum president Lorne Bozinoff rightly praised Rob's response to the storm, saying, "He was out and about during the ice storm, I think he did a good job . . . Every day he was somewhere and that works well."[8]

The ice storm was Rob at his best. He'd taken care of people face-to-face and spoke plainly to the public every day about what was going on. This was Rob Ford, mayor of Toronto, the way he was meant to be. And buoyed along by his success, Rob was front of the line on New Year's Day 2014 to register for re-election.

WITH 2014 UNDERWAY, our plan was to focus almost exclusively on Rob's re-election. To me, Rob seemed to be in high spirits. In an interview with *Esquire* magazine's Chris Jones, Rob had this to say about the upcoming election: "I don't want to call it a street fight. But I'll never back down. If the people want me to leave, on October 27th, they'll tell me to leave. But no councillors are going to tell me to leave. I know what I'm doing is right."[9]

By early March, we knew who those other contenders were. There was David Soknacki, who used to be a city councillor and who was a vocal proponent of LRTs over subways. The eccentric Sarah Thomson had also thrown her hat in the ring, running on a campaign of increased funding for the homeless. Karen Stintz filed her nomination papers in February; she was talking about a downtown subway relief line (although with her flip-flopping on transit issues when she'd served as chair of the TTC, who knew what she really intended to do). Then there was Olivia Chow, widow of the late Jack Layton, who'd stepped down from federal politics as an NDP MP to run against

Rob. Chow was being touted as the champion of the left-wing. Last but not least was John Tory, talking about transit and keeping taxes low and generally keeping everyone happy. Once again, the political establishment had their chosen one in the contest.

Rob wasn't worried about running against any of these people. In the same *Esquire* interview, he said he planned "to knock these guys out in the first 30 seconds."[10] Rob was fully confident he would beat John Tory hands down, knowing that he understood and appealed to the city's poorer neighbourhoods and visible minorities in a way Tory never would. When it came to Olivia Chow, Rob actually quite liked her, in much the same way he'd liked her husband. Despite media depictions, Rob knew that many of his supporters were also Chow's supporters, and vice versa. In fact, Rob told me he would have voted for Chow over Tory any day.

In terms of our campaign strategy, the plan we had for Rob was unchanged: knock on doors, meet people, return calls. It was as simple as that. In my personal opinion, the election *was* likely to be a street fight, but Rob was more than tough enough to take on the other people squaring off against him.

Around this time, a new video of Rob came out in public; this was a cellphone video taken at the Steak Queen restaurant in Rexdale, a place Rob went to pretty frequently. The video showed Rob, speaking in Jamaican patois, expressing his anger about Bill Blair and the ongoing police surveillance witch-hunt. It immediately drew a firestorm of controversy and outrage from all the usual suspects. To me, Rob's comments about Blair weren't the problem; his issues with the police chief had been going on long enough that what Rob had to say was pretty understandable. Rob's patois wasn't a problem either—it just showed how at home he was in Rexdale and with the Caribbean community (in fact, nobody in that community ever complained about being offended by Rob's patois). The problem was that the video showed him drunk again.

Even though I had believed Rob in the fall of 2013 when he told me—when he told the world—he'd quit drinking, I wasn't angry about the video. I will always believe that Rob was a better politician drunk or sober than the vast majority of people presently holding office in Toronto, if not the province and the country. I wasn't angry, but I was sad. And I was starting to worry in a way I hadn't before. I was starting to understand the extent of my brother's addiction and disease. Crack cocaine wasn't the issue; booze was.

"Devil's juice," as I like to call it, has destroyed more lives than any other drug. For the first time, I was coming to terms with the fact that Rob's life might be destroyed by devil's juice the same way so many others had been. I knew I would have to do something.

IN SPITE OF everything else going on—all the stress, all the craziness, the re-election campaign and my growing concern about Rob's alcoholism—Toronto was finally on the map. A major boost in tourism had already happened under Rob's leadership, before his substance-abuse problems came to light, but now we also had the added weight of various American late-night hosts. Chief among these was Jimmy Kimmel, who invited Rob down to LA to appear as a guest on his show in March 2014.

Randy and I both went with Rob. Rob, Randy and I shared the expenses for the trip. From the minute we hit the streets of LA, the whole experience was pretty surreal. Jimmy Kimmel himself picked us up. And from there, everybody down there seemed to already know who Rob was. We'd walk down the street and the tour buses would stop and people would jump out to get their pictures taken with him. Our friend Kevin O'Leary, of *Dragons' Den* and *Shark Tank* fame, was in LA at the same time, so we met up with him. Kevin was blown away by the attention Rob was getting, in a city already full of the biggest celebrities in the world. "Rob was just like a rock star," Kevin told us.

For our part, we had lots of fun, and as crazy as it all seemed, Rob would invite every person he saw back to Toronto. "Come to our beautiful city" was the invitation everyone on Hollywood Boulevard heard during our visit.

The actual interview with Kimmel took place on the evening of March 3. Rob got a huge round of applause when he walked out onstage. Kimmel didn't waste much time and put a lot of hard questions to Rob. Some people said Kimmel was even poking fun at him. But Rob took it all on the chin and kept it light. "I wasn't elected to be perfect," Rob said to Kimmel and the audience. "I'm just a normal, average, hard-working politician that's real, and I guarantee you call me, I will go to your front door."[11]

The interview wasn't long. TV interviews never are. Kimmel wanted to focus on all the scandal and get in as many jokes as he could, while Rob did his absolute best to promote Toronto. Maybe it was just a chance for Kimmel to mock Rob; on the other hand, there are plenty of people with marketing minds who say no media is bad media. I don't know if I agree with that, personally, and I would have rather had the opportunity come up in a more positive way, but before Rob Ford, people outside Canada had no idea what Toronto is all about and how great a city it is. Rob's personal issues aside, tourism in Toronto was booming, buildings were going up everywhere, and there was no negative impact on our economy. If anything, as far as the city's fortunes went, all of Rob's issues were having a positive impact. People from all over the world wanted to come and visit. LA proved that to us.

As for Jimmy Kimmel, he had this to say to Rob: "You are not the average politician, my friend . . . you are the most wonderful mayor I've ever witnessed in my many years in this job."[12] I'm sure a lot of people, Kimmel himself most likely, thought that was tongue-in-cheek, but at the same time, I think a lot of other people thought it was totally accurate.

As we moved into April, things were looking pretty good again. Rob made a friendly bet with Brooklyn borough president Eric Adams on who would win in the playoff series between the Toronto Raptors and the Brooklyn Nets. When Adams initially wagered beer, Rob countered with a CD of selected music from the losing leader's hometown. Adams accepted. On a sad note, April also saw the passing of Jim Flaherty. A state funeral was held at St. James Cathedral downtown. Rob was in attendance as one of the official delegates, alongside the prime minister and several other dignitaries. It was a good opportunity to leave politics aside for a little while.

I still had my worries about the extent of Rob's drinking, but his re-election was front and centre in our minds, and all efforts were going toward that. Back when he'd first run in 2010, the media had tried to tear him down by digging up stories from his past—the DUI in Florida, for example. That kind of muckraking had had the opposite effect, however, turning Rob into a real human being that people could relate to. Fast-forward to 2014, and the scandals—not to mention the relentless attacks from the media and the political establishment—were in some ways once again boosting Rob's humanity and relatability. On top of that, after we formally launched Rob's bid for re-election at the Toronto Congress Centre, we kept his campaign messages simple: subways, low taxes, financial management and accountability. These were subjects of far greater interest to the average taxpayer than what Rob Ford was doing in his personal time.

Meanwhile, the other mayoral contenders weren't coming across with the same clarity. As a CBC article put it, "Ford's rivals, meanwhile, must ask themselves if their campaigns can be explained as easily."[13] According to a Forum Research poll published in the middle of April, "The leading concern for voters in the upcoming election is sound economic management (21%), followed very closely by promoting jobs and growth and relieving the tax burden on the middle class (18% each)."[14] These were Rob's issues to a T, and though the same poll put Olivia Chow in the lead, there were plenty of people who believed Rob would win if the election were held right then and there.

Then came April 30. This time, it was *The Globe and Mail* publishing the story: "A second video of Toronto Mayor Rob Ford smoking what has been described as crack cocaine by a self-professed drug dealer was secretly filmed in his sister's basement early Saturday morning . . ."[15]

This time around, there had been another request for money by whoever had taken the video. *The Globe* hadn't paid for the video (apparently, the asking price was six figures), but they had purchased a number of screenshots, which they then published. Sure enough, Rob was smoking something in the pictures, but who really knew what was in the pipe? In fact, Rob's then-lawyer, Dennis Morris, had this to say: "If these guys are drug dealers and there's money involved, they can say whatever they want to get more money, to extract more money from the people who are paying . . . Would [*The Globe*] pay more for a video if I told you it was marijuana or crack cocaine?"[16]

A good question, but in a way it didn't matter. What did matter was that Rob had been drunk, very drunk, in Kathy's basement when that video was taken.

DIANE FORD

Rob wasn't much of a partier in high school. Not as far as I know. I remember he'd have some get-togethers here at our house. In fact, I always encouraged them to be here, so as the kids were growing up, everything happened here. I wanted to know what they were doing. But I never saw Rob drink. Not with his friends and not at family get-togethers. Doug Sr and I would have the odd drink, a glass of wine or cocktail at night. But other than that, our kids weren't brought up with a lot of liquor in the house. So Rob wasn't exposed to heavy drinking at home.

CHAPTER 21

Getting Help

I'm an alcoholic," said Rob in an interview with Bill Carroll, as I mentioned earlier. "I can't have one drink. It's like I have to have 100 or none . . . When you're in that sort of shape, or you're in that sort of mindset, you're really lonely, and you'll really hang on to anyone that will watch you do, or listen to what you have to say, and it's anyone at that time. It's just excuses. I'm not using excuses, I'm just being real with you. I just let a lot of people down. I've got thousands and thousands of hours and days and months to try to gain people's respect back, and maybe I've lost some forever. I can't change that, but hopefully some people will understand where I'm coming from and take it from there."[1]

Almost immediately after *The Globe and Mail* released the story and the screenshots, Rob came straight to me. He said, "Jones, I've got to get help."

Hearing this was a major weight off my shoulders, because my concern for him had come to a head, but here he was acknowledging it himself. We sat down and talked about it. For the first time, we really, openly talked about it. As I'd feared, the problem was the drinking. To the exclusion of all the other problems, it was the drinking. He revealed to me that by that time, he was drinking quite heavily every day and was very carefully keeping it hidden from me and the rest of the family. It broke my heart to hear all this. I could only wish I'd acknowledged it sooner. Maybe I could've done something about it.

"Enough's enough," said Rob.

"Okay," I replied. "Let's do this."

We wanted to act as quickly as we could. The first thing was to get Rob on a plane and take him down to a facility in California. Unfortunately, that didn't work out. Even though Rob didn't have a criminal record, US Customs decided to turn him away. I suspected there were some politics at play in that decision, but there wasn't any time to think about it. So we flew him back to Canada. I met him at Buttonville Airport, just north of Toronto. From there, we got him into a car and on the road to the GreeneStone facility up in Bala.

It was the middle of the night as we made our way up the highway. Throughout the drive, Rob spoke to his doctor on the phone. I listened in silence as he told the doctor what he'd told me: the extent of his drinking every day. More than anything else, I just felt sad, but as Rob owned up to everything to his doctor, I also had a chance to think about the whole picture.

Even if Rob had always been careful to not drink around me or our family, there's no denying that he enjoyed a few drinks from time to time. Sure, he had the DUI down in Florida all those years ago, but I think that was mostly a dumb mistake made by a young man. I don't mean that as an excuse of any kind, but I also don't think it was some major skeleton in his closet, or a major indicator of what was to come. It was a long time before Rob's drinking turned into full-blown alcoholism, and it wasn't even something that was a problem at the beginning of his mayoralty.

In my opinion, Rob really succumbed to alcoholism in 2013, particularly after Don Bosco fired him from his volunteer coaching position. Outside of his family, that coaching gig was the love of his life, more so even than politics. The kids on that team would call him with issues and problems, and it was a huge honour for him to be a mentor—in some cases a father figure—in their lives. Losing that role did him in like nothing else. That was the knife in the heart.

Now, Rob was fired from Don Bosco *after* the first crack allegations came out. I have no doubt that drinking played a key part in that incident, just as it had on St. Patrick's Day in 2012. It's important to remember how much pressure Rob was under when it came to the media and city council. For the most part, Rob always had had skin on him like an alligator. Other councillors could call him any name under the sun (as they had for the 14 years he'd been in municipal politics) and it would just roll off his back. Rob knew he was making positive changes all across the city. He felt the city had been in financial trouble when he took over, and he turned it around and left it with a surplus. He was rightfully proud of that, but there was still relentless hostility from certain quarters on council, not to mention the never-ending scrutiny from the media. All this is to say, if Rob blew off steam from time to time by drinking—even, unfortunately, drinking too much—that's somewhat understandable. Besides, his competence was never impaired by those incidents.

As for smoking crack, Rob said he was not an addict, and despite his deception about his drinking, I think that's true. I think he'd been caught in a compromised position a couple of times. He'd been lonely, stressed out and drunk. Someone—probably someone he trusted—put a pipe in front of him and he smoked it, not even thinking about it, certainly not realizing anybody was capturing him on video. It may sound naive of me to say this, but since Rob's death, I've had access to his financial records, and every penny was accounted for. He had no big, undetailed cash withdrawals—the kind of thing you'd associate with habitual drug purchases. Smoking crack, in other words, was a sideshow next to Rob's real illness.

In any case, as I sat in the car, listening to my brother, I knew the *pattern* of heavy drinking, the daily drinking, had happened after losing the Don Bosco football team. Council, media and threats were nothing compared to the heartbreak of that. From May 2013 onwards, my brother was badly hurt, and booze became his crutch. I don't think anyone from Don Bosco or anyone else could have foreseen that outcome.

Rob said, "To each his own, whatever you want to do . . . You want to drink? Go ahead, drink. You want to go smoke a joint, go ahead. It doesn't bother me, but I'm not going to sit here and be holier than thou, and don't do this and that. To me, personally speaking, I think alcohol is the worst drug ever."[2]

WITH ROB CHECKED into GreeneStone, there was nothing else to do but get back to the city and try to get a grip on everything. On May 1, I gave a press conference at city hall. I was exhausted, physically and emotionally, and it took all my effort not to break down as I spoke to the cameras and microphones. I didn't speak for very long. I told the media that the hardest thing about this was Rob acknowledging how many people he'd let down. I asked for everybody, regardless of political stripe, to keep him in their prayers and wish him a speedy recovery. And, maybe most importantly, I reminded them that everybody knows someone—maybe a friend or family member—who suffers from the disease of addiction. When I finished speaking, I didn't have the strength to take any questions.

The next few days, even the next few weeks, went by in a blur. Just because Rob was up at GreeneStone didn't mean the daily calls had stopped coming in to his office. I found myself trying to step up to answer them all. I actually don't know how he did it, being accessible to everyone in the city like that; I was running around like a chicken with my head cut off. From a city management perspective, there wasn't a lot that could get done in a month or two, especially with the mayor's powers and staff stripped down like it was. We had to do more with less, as the saying goes, but somehow we managed.

More broadly, the question of re-election had not been taken off the table for Rob at any point. There were definitely a lot of naysayers who thought rehab would mean Rob would drop out of the race. But many people also knew Rob was far from finished. A mid-May op-ed piece in *Maclean's* said this: "However steep the odds against him, Ford's past resilience makes him a marvel . . .

No surprise, then, that strategists for rival campaigns acknowledged this week that the 45-year-old remains very much part of their calculations."[3] Speaking from GreeneStone to the *Toronto Sun*, Rob had this to say: "I will be on the ballot for mayor in October, guaranteed, and . . . on October 28th, there will be no need to change the locks. There will be no need to clean out my office, because I am coming back."[4]

As far as the overall campaign went, Olivia Chow was leading in most of the polls, with Rob and John Tory tied for second place. Karen Stintz and David Soknacki were each in the single digits. Sarah Thomson wasn't even really on the radar, and I figured it wouldn't be long before she dropped out altogether. I was overseeing Rob's bid as his campaign manager. In June, there was a moment that seemed to surprise everybody when Olivia Chow and I publicly agreed that the municipal election process shouldn't be as long as it is (with registration in early January and the election itself in late October, the whole thing is almost a year). "There is no reason to have a municipal election that is 10 times longer than the provincial election," said Chow, adding that she thought four months, starting in July, would be sufficient.[5] Much to Chow's apparent surprise, I said, "This is going to be probably the one and only time you're going to hear Olivia Chow and I agree on anything . . . I don't think it takes the people of Toronto that long to figure out who they are voting for."[6]

Toronto's election wasn't the only one underway that summer, either. June also saw a provincial general election, after the NDP said it wouldn't support Kathleen Wynne's proposed budget. Since the Wynne Liberals were a minority government in the first place, they needed the added support of the NDP to get their agenda through; when that support fell apart, Ontarians found themselves at the polls. For better or worse, however, the Liberals won a majority in the 2014 general election, solidifying Kathleen Wynne's position as premier for the next four years. I couldn't help but wonder what new scandals might appear on the horizon.

Meanwhile, Rob was doing pretty well at GreeneStone. He didn't like it that much, to be honest, but then again, no one likes being in rehab. In addition to one-on-one counselling, there were also daily meetings in groups of eight or four. Rob told me that among the other residents were all sorts of professionals. It didn't matter what stature or how much money someone had; alcoholism and drug abuse crosses all walks of life. Of the treatment, Rob said, "At first, I was mad. I was mad at myself and saying, 'Why me?' . . . But then I realized it could have been a whole lot worse."[7] He was absolutely right. At GreeneStone, in addition to the counselling and therapy, he was working out every day, eating well and generally heeding the wake-up call he'd experienced in late April. I was very proud of him.

ROB CAME HOME from GreeneStone at the end of June. A couple of days later, he did an interview with CBC's Dwight Drummond. "I take full responsibility of what I've said, and what I've done," said Rob. "All I can do is apologize and deal with this disease. This is an everyday battle that I'm going to have to deal with for the rest of my life. It's the beginning of a long, long journey, and I'm going to battle this disease until the day I die . . . When you have this disease, you say things, you do things that aren't you . . . I wouldn't wish this disease on my worst enemy."[8]

I thought Rob looked a lot better. He'd lost some weight, and there was more colour in his face. We knew that those 60 days in rehab weren't enough to "cure" him, but as he said, it was the beginning of the long journey to becoming clean and sober. Another thing Rob said to Dwight Drummond was, "The person I was lying to the most was myself."[9] I'm glad he admitted that—deception was one of the worst parts of his alcoholism, but at last I felt as though I could take him at his word again, the way I'd always been able to before.

Rob had the campaign to focus on. He was fully aware of the competition he was facing from Olivia Chow and

John Tory. Rob also acknowledged that the last year in particular of his mayoralty had not gone well.

"I got elected," Rob told Bill Carroll, "and I was just on fire for the first 12 years of my political career. The last year as mayor, it just went south, but you know what? . . . I'm just up in the morning and I start returning calls as soon as I get in my car. I don't even wait until I get down to city hall . . . I don't know how many hours or days it's going to take me to build up the trust again, because I lied and connived to the whole world . . . I can't go around and apologize to everyone, but I thank people for calling. I can't thank people enough for their support and I just got to keep going one day at a time, because every day it gets easier and easier and easier, and I become more confident and more confident. It's easy to talk about, and I've never been happier in my life. Nothing can really bother me now. All the stuff that was something major, it's just minor after what I've gone through. I've gone, I've done it, I've been there. I've been here, there and everywhere, and now I'm here to help people out and I'll go anywhere."[10]

Helping people out and going anywhere, along with subways, customer service and fiscal management, was the backbone of Rob's campaign. In other words, it was back to basics. Signs and phone calls and knocking on doors. Rob was making a particular point of door-knocking and campaigning through subsidized housing, a community he'd always championed. If those folks got out to the polls in support of him, Rob's victory would pretty much be guaranteed.

As we moved through the summer, I was focused exclusively on managing the campaign. I'd been proud of representing Ward 2, Etobicoke North, but fortunately, my nephew Michael (Kathy's son) registered to run in July. Michael was only 20 years old at the time, but we had no doubt he'd be the third Ford to make his way onto Toronto city council. We knew he'd bring youth and optimism to the job, and we were very proud of him already.

In late July, we had that year's Ford Fest at a park in Scarborough. Thousands of people turned up and gave Rob their best wishes; it was a very moving display of solidarity and support. We had live music and tons of free food for everyone, but given the circumstances of Rob's last few months, we opted to keep the event alcohol-free. There were some people at city hall who objected to Ford Fest 2014, saying that we could potentially be using it as an unsanctioned campaign event. It was a ridiculous thing to worry about, since we'd been having Ford Fest for years—but it did prove to us that there were people still scrutinizing Rob's every move and waiting for him to make any kind of mistake.

Anyway, the highlight of that year's Ford Fest had to be Sarah Thomson showing up on a white horse. I believe she'd intended it to be some kind of event for her campaign, but it almost landed her a $100 ticket for violating municipal bylaws about riding horses in city parks. Thomson's bid for the mayoralty wasn't polling well; by August, she had less than 1 percent of support.[11] Not much later, Thomson dropped out of the mayor's race to run instead for a seat on council (she lost).

The other candidate to drop out before the end of the summer was Karen Stintz. She'd never managed to get her support much higher than 5 percent.[12] She stepped down fairly quietly, without endorsing any of the other candidates. Stintz also said that would be the end of her career in municipal politics and didn't seek to regain her seat on council. I've already said that we certainly had our differences with her, but Stintz had also been a councillor since 2003, and public service for that length of time should be commended.

On August 25, city council sat for the last time before the upcoming election. It was a pretty quiet, routine session (considering how some council sessions in the recent past had gone), without any really hot-button issues on the table. As soon as the session concluded, there was nothing left but to focus entirely on the campaign. We had only two months left to go. Most of the media was describing it as a bit of a four-way race. David Soknacki had risen in the polls; he was promoting a message of fiscal responsibility and clear policies. Meanwhile, Chow had her firm base with the downtown left-wingers. Tory, as usual, was touting his financial smarts but also trying to appeal to everyone. And then there was Rob, the guy with the proven track record, the guy who could relate to people of all political stripes, the guy who'd been knocked down, who'd picked himself back up, admitted his faults and was readier than ever to lead the city.

MICHAEL FORD

Rob had an illness. It was a very hard time for us. Addiction is in our family. My mother has addiction issues, as does my dad, so I saw a lot of it, growing up. Some of the stuff Rob did was inexcusable. I'm the first one to say that. And I told him many times, "Rob, come on, you need to start bringing it back. You need to get help." It was a battle for him to even hear that.

I don't think the media helped, either. They followed him day and night. It was as if they couldn't really go after his politics, because his politics were quite strong. That's not to say his politics were right or wrong, and not to say his politics weren't debatable, either, because they were. All politics are. He wasn't a traditional politician, and he struck some people the wrong way. But like it or not, his politics were strong. So certain members of the media had to use his personal downfalls to attack him, to get him off message. In that way, I think Rob was a victim to a certain extent. He was a man battling his demons in the limelight.

On the other hand, I find it difficult to put myself in his shoes and speculate on why he did what he did. I felt sorry for him. I don't think he was given the credit he was due for the good work he did for the city, and there was a lot of good work. But the trouble overshadowed it all.

Alcohol was the problem, but at the same time, Rob

Karla and me, and Rob and Renata, with Prime Minister Stephen Harper, his wife, Laureen, and their daughter, Rachel, at Harrington Lake, the prime minister's retreat, in 2011.

Rob arm-wrestled the legendary Hulk Hogan on August 23, 2013, and won their friendly match. Hulk had boasted that he would win and Torontonians would call him "Mayor Hogan" in victory, but Rob soon got the upper hand and shouted, "I own this town, man!" (Ernest Doroszuk, *Toronto Sun*, QMI Agency)

Rob was always self-conscious about his weight, and in 2008, he worked hard to get back into shape, though it was a struggle for him. Renata ran alongside her husband to motivate him.

Cutting the ribbon at the opening of a new playground. Olivia Chow (in red), a political opponent who supported Rob during some of his darkest times, lends a hand. Rob worked hard to support children of all backgrounds, especially new Canadians.

Team Ford supporting the Toronto Maple Leafs at the construction of a local outdoor rink in 2012.

Rob having a laugh with Toronto Raptors ambassador Drake while announcing that Toronto had been granted the 2016 NBA All-Star Game, September 30, 2013. (Photo by Frank Gunn/Canadian Press)

Rob with Donald Trump at the ribbon-cutting ceremony for Trump International Hotel and Tower in Toronto, April 16, 2012. Some in the media have compared Trump to Rob, but Rob was one of a kind.

Rob and me with Hazel McCallion, the former mayor of Mississauga, on Mother's Day, 2014, at Topiarys Restaurant. Hazel was the longest serving mayor in Canadian history, but Rob may have challenged her record had fate not intervened.

Greeting a young Ford supporter.

A fan embraces Rob at Ford Fest in Scarborough in 2013. (Aaron Vincent Elkaim/*National Post*)

By 2013, Rob was well on his way to becoming a celebrity, and despite his personal challenges, his fans came out to see him in droves. (Associated Press)

At Ford Fest with boxing legend George Chuvalo. (Craig Robertson/*Toronto Sun*)

A lighter moment at city hall, with Amin Massoudi. Amin joined our team right out of Queen's University and worked with Rob when he was a councillor, before he became mayor. He was Rob's most trusted and closest staffer, and a good friend. (David Cooper/*Toronto Star* via Getty Images)

Shopping with Stephanie and Dougie. The media scrutinized Rob's every move, even when he was with his family. (Ernest Doroszuk/*Toronto Sun*)

Jimmy Kimmel invited the Ford boys to his show in Los Angeles at the height of the media frenzy and even picked us up from the airport. Rob had become the most famous mayor in the world.

The Rob Ford bobbleheads were a huge hit with his supporters. Crowds would line up for hours, and Rob would sign one for everyone, with the proceeds going to the Humber River Hospital.

In 2014, Rob geared up for re-election as mayor, and he would have won, too, if he hadn't become ill with cancer. (Reuters)

In the last days of Rob's life, nothing meant more to him than his family. Renata, Dougie and Stephanie miss Rob very much. Thousands turned out in the rain for the visitation at Toronto City Hall, and every seat was taken for the funeral at St. James Cathedral, March 30, 2016.

Members of the Don Bosco football team came down to Toronto City Hall to pay their respects to Rob and our family, March 28, 2016. (Laura Pedersen, *National Post*)

Rob Ford, May 28, 1969–March 22, 2016. (Steve Russell/*Toronto Star* via Getty Images)

wasn't a man to take a break. He worked very hard. He didn't stop working, early in the morning to late at night. He wasn't one to go take a vacation, to go clear his head for a few days. But you can only go so far working like that, so I think that kind of work and the stress that comes with it were a big part of what triggered the alcoholism.

I've learned some lessons from Rob. For starters, I think I have a much healthier respect for my work and private life balance. I make sure that once every three or four weeks, I take a weekend. I'm a pilot. I love flying. I'll go to the island airport and go for a flight. There's nothing better than flying over the city of Toronto in a sunset. That clears my mind. So I think I've found my passion in terms of being a politician, but I've also found the balance. Did Rob balance it? Did he take the breaks he should've taken? No, he didn't. I wish he had. I'm also very cautious about alcohol, having seen what Rob and other members of my family have gone through.

DIANE FORD

I didn't know anything about Rob's drinking incidents until I saw it on television. And then I would sort of justify it—everybody's got a different way of unwinding, and that was his way. Nobody in their right mind could sit and take the abuse that he took, and do the job that he did, without some unwinding. So that's how I justified the drinking incidents after I found out about them. I also had enough faith in him that he'd use some common sense . . . but it was an addiction, and I didn't realize it at first.

I had no idea what to make of the video about the drugs. I was sick about it, that the media was talking about it to start with. Nobody saw the video at first, so I wondered if there was even any truth to it. I thought maybe it was just a fabricated story, because sensationalism really sells papers. Rob was a well-known person, after all, and there were lots of people out to attack him. So when all this was coming up, I was not questioning him, but I was questioning myself. I was really mixed up. But then came the day that he actually admitted it, doing those drugs, and I just about fell over. It suddenly dawned on me that a lot of things were true after all. It was devastating.

Rob went to rehab in the summer of 2014. I didn't visit him at GreeneStone, but I did go up and meet him in the nearby town. He wanted some new suits, because he'd lost weight and was feeling good, and he'd always wanted me to help him pick new clothes. I'd always been concerned about his weight; it was also part of his addiction. When he finished the rehab program, I was really happy, but as he came back to Toronto, I wasn't sure if he was going to win the re-election. A lot of damage had been done. A lot. I know he was his own person. I know he was responsible for these things. I blame the media for a lot, but Rob was also stupid. I hate using that word, because overall he was not a stupid man, but he did stupid things. I think it was because of alcohol that he would be in the company of people who would take a picture of him and try to sell it. If he couldn't see that, I don't know what was wrong with him.

RENATA FORD

Rob wasn't a chronic drinker or a chronic drug addict. But with the constant pressure of the media, and the endless scrutiny, and the chief of police saying he was disappointed, it all got to Rob. He was a human being. These days, the media talks about bullying a lot—the bullying of children, the bullying of certain groups of people. Well, what about the media's bullying of my husband? Whether he had weaknesses or not, it went too far. That's bullying too.

Everyone has their vices, but he always seemed quite sober when he came home. He would usually go straight to bed, because it was almost always late at night. I understood from the beginning that the hours were going to be long.

I think rehab was hard on him because he'd always thought he had things under control. But he needed that help, no matter how much he'd defied getting help before. He needed that time away to reflect on everything. He came to realize there wasn't much point to life if he was going to be out of control or giving in to his addictions all the time.

CHAPTER 22

The Diagnosis

On the morning of September 10, Rob and I met for breakfast at Perkins Restaurant in Rexdale. We had the usual things to discuss, mostly campaign-related. With only 50-odd days left until the election, there was a slate of upcoming debates that were bound to be heated. Rob had done very well in debates against George Smitherman back in 2010, and there was no reason to think he couldn't perform just as well this time around.

But for some reason, that morning, his head didn't seem to be in the game. Finally, I asked him what was wrong.

"I don't know," said Rob. "I've got a stomach ache right now. It's not bad right now, but it was really painful overnight. Kept me awake most of the night."

I sat back, considering what he'd just said. I knew he'd been keeping totally clean. He wasn't drinking; he wasn't doing any drugs. He was keeping up with his post-rehab counselling and he was looking good. More than that, he was *feeling* good . . . at least until that morning. On the other hand, back in 2011, Rob had been treated for kidney stones. Anyone who's had kidney stones knows how excruciating they can be; dealing with them for any longer than necessary would take away from the focus Rob needed for the campaign.

"Why don't we go get you checked out?" I said.

I thought Rob might object—he had a habit of always wanting to tough it out—but to my surprise he nodded. "Yeah," he said. "Let's go."

He went to see his doctor, who sent us on to Humber River Hospital. Rob's stomach ache had intensified again, so the folks at Humber put him through a battery of tests, including a CAT scan, as soon as we got there. I was still thinking it was kidney stones at that point—a CAT scan is a pretty normal procedure for diagnosing stones, after all. At the same time, I knew we always had at least one or two members of the media somewhere on our tail, so it wouldn't be long before people knew that Rob had gone to the hospital that morning. Still, Rob was healthy, feeling great and in fighting form. We didn't *really* have anything to worry about . . .

It wasn't even noon when the CEO of Humber River, Dr. Rueben Devlin, came out to see us. Dr. Devlin was a family friend; he had served as president of the PC Party under Mike Harris, and we'd known him for years. He asked us to accompany him into a small office away from the main part of the hospital. The three of us sat down, Dr. Devlin, Rob and me. The office, I remember, was small, only about eight feet by eight feet. For some reason, it felt a little claustrophobic.

"Rob," said Dr. Devlin, "I've got bad news. There are spots on your chest and stomach. We'll need to send your tests down to Mount Sinai right away so that we can confirm it, but I believe you have cancer."

WHEN ROB SPOKE to Bill Carroll, he was kind of philosophical about his diagnosis. He said, "I guess the good Lord gave me this to say, 'Here, you want to mess around? We'll mess around.' That's when I really woke up. And after rehab, I thought, 'Okay, good. Things are going good.' Until whammo, one day I told my brother, 'I just don't feel good.' . . . I went one day to Humber and [they] put me into the CAT scan and said—I'll never forget, my brother was there—you've got cancer."[1]

I was a lot less philosophical about it. In fact, I was in a state of utter shock. Sometimes life hits us like a whirlwind, and within half a day, everything changes. It felt like I'd been having breakfast with him one minute, and he was telling me about his stomach pains, and I was thinking it was kidney stones. Then the next minute, I was knocked flat. Still, things needed to be done right away. From the outset, even before they sent his tests to Mount Sinai for confirmation, Rob said he wasn't going to step down from the race. The CT scan at Humber River had just turned up spots. Scary? Yes, but there's a lot of survival in cancer—and there was a lot of fight and determination in Rob Ford.

So as Rob was moved into a bed in a room at Humber River, I had to put my shock aside to make some kind of statement to the media. At least he'd been in high spirits; I would try to focus on his energy to keep me going. The campaign team and I hastily put together a press conference. We held it right there at the hospital. Fortunately, Dr. Devlin stayed on hand the whole time. He was able to speak about the medical specifics of Rob's diagnosis.

It didn't take long before I found myself once again surrounded by cameras and microphones, speaking on my brother's behalf. I tried to keep my voice steady as I related the events of that morning at Perkins and confirmed that Rob had been diagnosed with a tumour. I thanked all the well-wishers, who'd already started to flood our phones and email accounts, and I asked the media to give our family some space for the time being. As before, I didn't bring politics into it, and I kept my comments short. I couldn't trust myself to keep it together anyway. After I spoke, Dr. Devlin stood up to offer his analysis: "A CT scan is very definitive for the tumour. It wasn't a small tumour, but the size is not as relevant as what it is . . . We really need a biopsy."[2]

By this point, it was suppertime, and for the moment, there wasn't much we could do but wait for the biopsy results. Our family knew by now, as well, and had joined us at the hospital to be by Rob's side. We were all maintaining a sense of confidence and optimism.

Whatever was going to happen would happen; for now, Rob just needed to rest.

THE WHIRLWIND WAS not finished with us, and the official diagnosis from Mount Sinai came back in about 24 hours. It wasn't good. Rob had pleomorphic liposarcoma, a rare and very aggressive kind of cancer that develops quickly in muscle, bone and fat tissues.

Right away, the question was how Rob could beat this thing. We didn't even use the word *if*. In any case, Dr. Walter Longo, a professor of surgery from Yale University quoted in the *Toronto Star*, said, "If they can get all the disease out surgically . . . he'll have about a 50/50 chance of beating it."[3] Rob's doctor at Mount Sinai, Zane Cohen, was optimistic about the treatments. No matter what, though, we were looking at a stiff regimen of chemotherapy. And every ounce of Rob's energy was going to be needed to fight the battle for his health.

As soon as we got a break from the doctors and the hard conversations, I went in and sat by Rob's bedside. We were both silent for a little while. Then Rob looked me in the eye and said, "Doug, there's something I need you to do . . ."

THE NEXT DAY, September 12—barely 48 hours after that breakfast at Perkins—we released a statement to the media. The statement was Rob's and Rob's alone, and here it is in full:

As many of you know, I've been dealing with a serious medical issue, the details of which are unknown. But I know that with the love and support of my family, I will get through this.

I want to thank the residents of Toronto for your wishes and prayers and I also want to thank the amazing staff at Humber River Hospital and Mount Sinai Hospital for the care and compassion you have shown not just me but all the people who come here to get better.

People know me as a guy who faces things head on and never gives up, and as your mayor, I have done just that. I derailed the gravy train, cut unnecessary spending and made government more accountable. I did this by facing these challenges head on.

Now I could be facing a battle of my lifetime, and I want the people of Toronto to know that I intend to face this challenge head on and win.

With the advice of my family and doctors, I know I need to focus on getting better. There is much work to be done and I can't give it my all at this point in time.

My heart is heavy when I tell you that I'm unable to continue my campaign for re-election as your mayor.

While I'm unable to commit to the heavy schedule required for a mayoral candidate, I will not turn my back on Ward 2. I will be running as councillor of Ward 2, to represent the fine folks that have become my neighbours and friends over these past 14 years.

Four years ago, we made history. With your help, we started a movement that would take back our city.

I was not alone in this; my big brother Doug was by my side, sharing my vision, fighting for the great people of Toronto. I never could have accomplished what we did without him.

Doug loves our city as much as I do. He believes that standing up for the average person and watching the bottom line are what matters most at city hall.

Doug also believes in standing up for his family no matter what. His loyalty and willingness to be there for anyone, anytime is just who he is.

I've asked Doug to finish what we started together, so that all we've accomplished isn't washed away.

I have asked Doug to run to become the next mayor of Toronto, because we need him. We cannot go backwards.

I love our city and I love being your mayor. It has been an honour and a privilege to serve you.

For the past four years, I have gotten up every day thinking about our great city and how to make life just a little bit better for each of you.

To anyone facing a serious health challenge, I wish you strength and courage on your journey; you are not alone.

Hope is a powerful thing. With hope, support and determination, I know I will beat this, not just for my family, but for YOU, Toronto.

My family and I thank you for your continued support and prayers. God bless.[4]

—Rob Ford

Needless to say, the whirlwind that had picked up our lives was *still* blowing. *The Globe and Mail* called it a "stunning last-minute reversal."[5] In many ways, actually, no one was more stunned than I was. Anyway, there was no time to waste. September 12 was a Friday, and the cut-off for all registrations was at 2:00 p.m. I hustled down to city hall with Jeff Silverstein, who'd been serving as Rob's campaign communications director. Everything was a frenzy, and I didn't even have the $200 on me to pay for the registration—I had to ask John Nunziata (Councillor Frances Nunziata's brother) to loan me the money. As soon as we'd squared that paperwork away, we put in the paperwork for Rob's formal withdrawal from the mayor's race. Our nephew, Michael, also withdrew, so that Rob could run once again as a councillor back in Ward 2, Etobicoke North. Michael intended to run as a trustee for the school board. With that done, I gave my own statement to the media, confirming that this was something Rob had asked me to do. Once again, I asked for everyone to keep Rob in their thoughts, as he was keeping them in his.

The reaction in the establishment media to my candidacy was pretty quick, and, I guess, pretty predictable. Some people wanted to suggest that my taking Rob's place as mayor was part of our secret Ford plan all along. The very same day I registered—September 12—*The Globe and Mail* ran an article saying, "The idea of Doug Ford stepping in to take his brother's place has been in the air for some time and those who were once close to the mayor's office say it was floated more than a year ago . . ."[6]

Once again, "unknown sources" had "leaked" the idea that we might have a "secret plan" to the media, but it was complete bullshit. I wasn't even going to run for council again, let alone the mayoralty. The only Ford for the job, as far as I was concerned, was Rob. When he'd asked me in the hospital to take his spot in the race, I'd almost laughed. But he was dead serious about it, and there was no way I could say no to him. In the frantic last few hours, I hadn't had a chance to have a serious conversation with my wife and daughters about it. I also definitely hadn't had time to switch my focus from running Rob's campaign to running my own.

In terms of the other front-runners, Olivia Chow didn't make any comments off the top other than to continue offering her best wishes for Rob. John Tory, on the other hand, was quick to take some swipes at me. He called me "maybe worse" than my brother and also said that I was an "insult machine."[7] I didn't really know what either of those comments were supposed to mean, but I didn't really care either. I was doing this for Rob and the city, and if Tory wanted to drop the gloves, I was more than happy to oblige.

FROM THE MOMENT I filed the registration to run, I knew my bid for mayor would be an uphill battle. I had six weeks to go, which in many ways was just four weeks, because it took two weeks to switch over all the campaign literature and signs and get properly reorganized. It wasn't much time to get it together. Still, I thought we were doing extremely well, considering the circumstances. I would start at six in the morning and go until midnight every single day, knocking on doors, getting our message out there, rallying support. In a smaller city, I believe I would've hit every house on every street.

I didn't really have a campaign manager, per se. I had Jeff Silverstein handling communications, and I had Rob's long-time staffer Amin Massoudi giving his tireless support as well. I didn't receive any endorsements. I think a lot of other politicians, even our allies, got cold feet and ran for the hills. In the meantime, it took me a few weeks of campaigning to differentiate myself from Rob. That's not a knock against him; in my opinion, he will always be the best guy for the job. He'd run circles around me. But I was a little different, and I needed to prove my differences.

During this time, Rob's treatments had begun. He took a break from the hospital and made it down to city hall on October 2, even giving some comments to the media while he was there. "I'd like to just cry myself to sleep," he said, "but what can you do? There's only so many tears that can be shed, and you just have to move on."[8] He also added that a lot of his past problems, he knew, were self-inflicted, but his cancer was not. At the time, the doctors knew how truly severe his sickness was, but we all worked very hard to keep the details private. I couldn't even really think about it, to be honest, or I would fall apart.

Meanwhile, the race for the mayor's seat went on. According to the polls, Olivia Chow had slipped out of the lead. (She was right, I believe, when she'd said the campaign is way too long; it seemed as if her popularity had burned itself out a bit in the home stretch.) John Tory had taken over, and through October, I was polling only a few points behind him. But in the end, it wasn't enough. The establishment had their man in Tory, and this time around, they'd thrown their full weight behind him. On October 27, John Tory was elected as the city's next mayor.

I was disappointed for my campaign team, small and lean as it was. They did an incredible job. We finished in second place on election night, with 330,000 votes (to Tory's 394,000 and Chow's 226,000). The city had had a record voter turnout that year, and I was disappointed for all the folks who'd voted for me. Privately, I hate losing. Even something as small as a game of checkers, I hate losing. But we just didn't have enough time, and that was that.

Outside of my campaign for mayor, Michael won his school trustee position, securing his entry into municipal politics, and Rob easily won his old seat in Etobicoke North. In a way, it kind of felt like things were coming around in a circle for him, for all of us. It was a time for Rob in particular to take a bit of a step back and really devote himself to his battle with cancer. In his mind, the mayor's seat would open up again in 2018, and he had every intention of winning it once again. I wholeheartedly supported him, and I told him I'd be with him every step of the way.

On November 30, 2014, my brother's time as mayor of Toronto came to an end.

MICHAEL FORD

I think Rob came back from GreeneStone ready to go. I also think an addiction is something that you live with; in other words, he didn't beat it, but he had it under control. He understood that. I'd gone to visit him on weekends, and as he went through the treatment, I could see how his mindset was changing. I think he realized that once an addict, always an addict, and from then on, he knew he couldn't mess up. If he had one drink, he'd be up shit's creek. He very much turned his life around in that respect.

He came back energized, but he also had a mountain to climb, in terms of re-election. I was right beside him. I was always in the campaign office, with Doug as well. Rob was focused and had a good team around him. He still had a massive following in the public that had never left him either. They stuck by him. People like the underdog. People like seeing a turnaround. In a way, it was part of the populist movement. It wasn't a Conservative thing, wasn't Liberal, wasn't NDP. Rob appealed to people of all walks of life, of all ethnicities. They wanted to see him get back.

Then came that day in September. I was at the campaign office with our staff and Rob was missing in action. We didn't know what was going on. I didn't even know. I tried calling Doug, but he wasn't answering. I didn't want to tell the volunteers anything. The first thing that had come into my mind was, "Has Rob had a relapse? Was he out drinking last night?" I was very involved in the operations at the campaign offices, both in Scarborough and Etobicoke, so that kept me busy every minute.

Then finally, around three or four o'clock, I got a call from my mother. Through tears, she said, "It's really bad. I need you to pick me up."

All I could say was "Okay, oh my God, what's going on?" I thought something serious had happened. An accident maybe.

I went from the campaign office straight to my mother's house, picked her up, and we went back to the family house on Weston Wood. My grandmother was devastated, but she was able to at least give us some of the details. We didn't know then that he had cancer, but there was a 99 percent chance of it, according to the chief of staff at Humber hospital. They were about to transfer Rob down to Mount Sinai.

That night, it was like a bomb had hit. My grandmother was beside herself. So was my mom. Doug was mostly silent, trying to think about the whole thing. So I tried to be the optimistic one. I said, "Guys, relax, we don't know anything. We don't know where this is at. Is it good? No. But let's relax until we know more."

I ended up going back to the campaign office, and then when I walked into my office, I got very emotional. I had two of our most senior people in there—I'd pulled them in just to let them know what was going on. They too had wondered if Rob had had a relapse with drinking or drugs, but when I was able to get myself together and tell them it was probably cancer, they were in total disbelief.

The next morning, we went back to Humber hospital. The place was surrounded by the media. I'll never forget that—the whole hospital circled by reporters and news crews. Anyway, I remember going in to see Rob. I'd never seen him look so stunned. He already knew he was in the fight of his life. He just knew it. Part of it was knowing that my grandfather—Doug Sr—had died of cancer too, only 10 years earlier. That scared the shit out of Rob—knowing he was possibly facing the very same thing.

I'll never forget looking at his face at that moment, in that hospital room.

CHAPTER 23

Saying Goodbye

For the first few months of 2015, Rob's life was ruled by his chemotherapy treatments. The goal was to shrink the tumour in his abdomen enough so that it could be removed. It was sarcoma, which scared him, but the family and I knew we needed to stay optimistic. So I kept telling him, "You're going to make it. Just stay positive." By May, it looked as if the tumour had shrunk enough to be removed. It was a very long, hard procedure. This is how Rob described his experience: "It was hard. I have a high tolerance. In the hospital, I had excruciating pain. They cut me 12 inches, from just under my breast plate, right down to my groin. They cut me again from the left to the right about—I think it was 14 inches. So basically, it was a T upside down."[1]

DIANE FORD

Doug phoned me and told me what was going on at Humber hospital. It was very serious, Doug told me. At first, I couldn't even talk about it. I just hung up the phone. We made arrangements to take Rob down to Mount Sinai. I went in the ambulance with him. He didn't say a word, but there were tears running down his cheeks. He knew then. He knew in his heart that it was bad. But we were all optimistic. We kept thinking about the chemo. We hoped and prayed and spent every day at the hospital.

They shrunk the tumour first. It was encouraging, because the shrinking worked. Otherwise, they wouldn't have been able to operate and remove it, so there was more reason to be optimistic. Then Rob had to heal, so he wasn't doing any more chemo at that point. Over the next 12 months or so, it was a roller coaster ride, but there was lots to be hopeful about.

The surgery knocked Rob out of commission for a few months, but in general, he was feeling a lot better. His hair started to grow back, and he was able to return to work. As we went through the summer and into the fall, there was even reason to believe that Rob might be out of the woods. The interview Rob did with Bill Carroll—which has been so instrumental in capturing how Rob felt about a lot of things—happened on October 1, 2015. Although I've quoted from that interview throughout this book already, I think there are a few more of Rob's comments that fit well here.

ROB FORD

I spend [evenings] with my kids. I go to their soccer games—they all play soccer—and I do a lot of studying with them . . . [Before,] it wasn't a very good scene. Thankfully, I don't think they saw that, because I was coming home five, six in the morning. It's a completely different atmosphere [now]. My whole life has changed. That's why I'm saying somebody upstairs has done this, purposefully, because . . . between you and I, I would have been dead for sure how I was going. Would have been dead by now without the cancer. The alcohol and the drugs—would have been dead. My heart wouldn't have taken it. The cancer indirectly might have saved my life. Pretty sure of that.[2]

In that same interview with Bill Carroll, Rob had also said he had no new tumours. If only that were true. A couple of weeks after the interview, Rob had new abdominal pains, so he went in for a checkup. The doctors did some tests, including CT scans. The results were not good. Rob's cancer had reappeared, this time on his bladder. He was looking at two rounds of chemo at least, before the end of the year.

As news of Rob's new tumour spread, I soon had people from all over the country calling us up with different remedies and solutions. If they weren't calling me or another member of my family, they were calling Mount Sinai. But there wasn't much for Rob to do but go on with the chemo again, hard on him as it was. He lost his hair again, and he had to wear a loose-fitting track suit whenever he got out of the house or the hospital.

Through all that time, he never, ever stopped returning phone calls.

Around this same time, part of Rob's treatment regimen was something we called the "mouse trial." Dr. Rochelle Schwartz and her husband, Yaron Panov, who was also battling liposarcoma, had raised over $1 million for research after a mouse trial had prolonged Panov's life by several years. As I understood it, doctors would take a biopsy of Rob's cancer, inject it into laboratory mice and then treat the mice with different chemotherapies to see which one worked best. The mouse trial was still in the experimental stages, but it seemed like a much more accurate way of finding the right chemo for Rob's cancer. Rob was incredibly grateful to Dr. Schwartz and Mr. Panov, and to Dr. Albiruni Ryan Abdul Razak, the doctor who was leading the study.

The mouse trial was the last bit of hope we had, and for a little while, there seemed to be a slim chance Rob might pull through again. In January 2016, he even made it out to a hockey game, where he said to the *Toronto Sun*'s Joe Warmington, "I feel much better . . . I am on my way back."[3]

Unfortunately, we didn't have enough time for the mouse trial to be 100 percent complete. Rob was only getting sicker and sicker. He was living at home and had nurses coming in. He couldn't get out of bed, couldn't even go to the washroom, and by the end of February, we knew the end was pretty near. The time had come for him to move from home into the hospital.

RENATA FORD

The cancer was very difficult. All the doctors told me I needed to stay positive with him. As we got to the end, Rob realized how much he didn't want to leave us. The point of his life was his family, but it was too late. Toward the very end, he just worried about us. That's what I remember most from his last days—his just being worried about us.

DIANE FORD

I went to Florida, because I had to go and check on the house we had down there, and there wasn't much I could do in Toronto. I was planning on staying a month, and I thought if anything started going downhill, I'd come back. But I didn't really think that way, because we were looking at experimental drugs, the mice tests and everything. As it turned out, I was only in Florida for two weeks when I got an email from Doug. The doctors had done a new round of CAT scans and had found the cancer had spread. There was going to be a meeting at the hospital the next morning, and the doctors said it would be wise to have the whole family around. I knew that was it. I packed my bag and I was on the plane that night.

So once again, we were all at the hospital taking turns and doing everything we could. Michael slept there. So did Randy. Doug was there morning, noon and night. I bought Rob a lounge chair, a great big, comfy recliner. If he touched a button on the armrest, that chair would almost eject him. Doug and Rob and I were in hysterics one day, because the chair just about shot Rob across the hospital room. A couple of nights he slept in the chair, because he was really uncomfortable a lot of the time.

This one day, Rob had terrible pains in his stomach. He was on a lot of painkillers, too. The nurse said, "When you get these pains, Rob, this is what you do," and she showed him how to rub his stomach in a particular way to ease the discomfort. After she'd gone out of the room, Rob asked me to rub his stomach the way the nurse had been doing it. I said okay, and I started rubbing. At first, he told me to go clockwise, but pretty quickly he changed his mind and told me to go the other way. No sooner had I started rubbing counter-clockwise when he told me to go clockwise again.

"For Christ's sake, Rob," I said, "make your mind up, will you?"

He started laughing at that, and I started laughing. We were trying to make light of everything. That was the last laugh we had together.

The doctors and nurses and hospital staff were all really good, but they knew. I think they had known for about six months before that it was hopeless for him. As things went further downhill, he just slept all the time. It was almost like he was in a coma, but he wasn't. He'd open his eyes, try to talk. We'd give him ice chips, and he'd want a drink. They said he couldn't have a drink, but if I'd known how close it was to the end, I would have given him what he wanted. At that point, what did it matter what was going in and going out of him?

Right up until the very end, we still had hope. False hope it was, but hope all the same.

After Rob was moved into palliative care at Mount Sinai, he didn't want to talk to anyone for the first little while. He wanted no visitors whatsoever outside of family. Then one day, out of the blue, I happened to run into David Miller in the elevator. We chatted for a short while, and then it occurred to me to ask him if he might want to visit Rob. Rob had always really liked David, and even though he didn't want visitors overall, I thought David might brighten things up for him. They ended up having a good visit, David and Rob, and I knew Rob was glad I'd brought David around.

Then a couple days later, John Tory called to see if he could come by. He came with Denzil Minnan-Wong and Councillor Steve Holyday (Doug Holyday's son). It was good of them to visit, although it was an especially hard time for me. The day before, in fact, the doctors had been talking to Rob about his resuscitation wishes if he went into a coma. That weighed pretty heavily on me, and I couldn't stop thinking about it. At the end of the visit with Tory, Minnan-Wong and Holyday, Rob said, "God bless you," as his visitors walked out the door. I made it into the hallway before breaking down in front of them. I'd held it together until then, but I couldn't contain it anymore.

Our whole family was at the hospital around the clock. The doctors kept telling us Rob only had a few days left, but Rob kept hanging on, fighter that he was. For the last five days of his life, Rob slept. He only opened his eyes twice during that time. The first time happened when his kids came in the room to see him, about three days before he passed. His eyes popped open at the sound of their voices. He even managed to say, "Wow. Hey, guys, how are you? I love you." I had to leave the room when that happened—it was another thing that did me in, just like Rob's parting words to John Tory and his other visitors.

On the last day, Michael, Randy and I were in the room with Rob. It was mid-morning. His breathing had become very bad, and he constantly needed to have fluid removed from his airway. Otherwise, nothing much had changed. All of a sudden, he opened his eyes wide and looked straight at me. He hadn't opened his eyes since his kids had visited. But there he was, looking at me. I was face to face with him, looking back at him. My mother and Renata came into the room at that very moment. I couldn't let go of him. I just held on to him as he breathed his last breath.

Then it was over. Rob was gone. I held on to him for a long time, for as long as I could, sobbing all the while. I'd lost my brother and my best friend, and life would never be the same.

* * *

In the days after Rob's passing, the whole family felt empty. We had to make all the arrangements for the funeral, however, and John Tory was a huge help to us. He treated our family extremely well and bent over backwards to help us, as Rob had done for Jack Layton when he passed away in 2011. The service for Rob was held on the morning of March 30. We started with a funeral procession from city hall to St. James, and I'll never forget the folks lined up along the way, singing "Amazing Grace" and "When the Saints Go Marching In." Among them were many of Rob's football players, all wearing their jerseys, linked to each other hand-in-hand. Rob loved those kids, and it was overwhelming to have them there with us.

As for Rob's funeral itself, the city staff—especially those in protocol—were incredible. The honour guards from the police, the fire department, EMS and the TTC all volunteered their time, as did the folks at St. James Cathedral, including Reverend Andrew Asbil. I also felt tremendous gratitude to Premier Kathleen Wynne for attending the service. We've had many political differences over the years, but she put those differences aside and came to pay her respects. She didn't have to do that. And I have to say that Chief Mark Saunders, who also attended the funeral, is a great chief, and we have a great deal of respect for him. He is a very humble man and a cops' cop.

The front-line police officers love him. The outpouring of support that followed Rob's passing truly helped us get through that difficult time.

We also had the privilege of hearing or reading thousands and thousands of tributes to Rob. The tributes came in letters and cards and emails. Some remarks were spoken at his funeral. Some were spoken in the media. I think these tributes tell the story of my brother as many other people saw him, so I've included a few here.

CLINTON LEONARD

FOOTBALL PLAYER COACHED BY ROB FORD

I would like to thank everyone for coming out today. I'm sure the family greatly appreciates you all . . . The team and I are still heartbroken that Coach is really gone. He'll be truly missed. Coach was always about family and gelling as a unit. With that came our team memorable moments, with us going to Peterborough to play an exhibition game, then staying at a hotel. Coach told all of us to be on our best behaviours, or "you guys are going to run and do six inches until practice [is] over." No one wanted to get that face red, so we behaved, but Coach still believed somebody would [do] something stupid. So he pretty much hid in the bushes, looking for us.

Another great memory was after each season, he would take . . . all of us to Pizza Hut for lunch on Kipling. I would—I could be here all day telling you guys what Coach did for all of us. He was honestly a blessing. He showed us right from wrong and steered us onto the right paths to be smart, successful young men in today's society. Rest in sweet paradise, Coach Ford. We love you.[4]

REX MURPHY

"God must have loved the common man. He made so many of them." Words of the wisest of presidents, Abraham Lincoln. And part of Lincoln's wisdom was that he looked with unabbreviated appreciation upon ordinary men and women, the multitude of everyday people for whom life is hard, work relentless, disappointments many.

Well, the common man lost a buddy yesterday. Rob Ford, the impresario mayor of Toronto, fell to an unconquerable cancer. Mr. Ford was one of the most remarkable ordinary people Toronto has ever produced. He deserved the critical press he got—he was Toronto's mayor, after all—but he did not deserve the zest and vicious scorn some brought to the coverage of him. His hard times and personal failings called up, from some, a blitz of mockery and derision that had in it at least as much snobbery as righteousness. There was far more kindness in Rob Ford than in the most zealous of those who couldn't stand him, and a stronger pulse of compassion in those who did stay by him than those who found delight in his many failings and follies.

To say he was flawed is both understatement and redundant. We all are. But Mr. Ford was the bull in his own china shop. He did strain the loyalty he inspired. He was reckless. Sometimes distemperate. But at the core, the man was something larger than all the flaws. He had a sense of the flow and pattern of everyday lives. There was no gap between him and those on the outside of privilege and station. His language might be rough and some of his comments jam the radar of political correctness. But he was more at ease, more natural and welcoming, to the many faces and tones of Toronto's multicultural mix than many of its more ostentatious champions. The annual Ford party out in the wilds of Etobicoke was like a chicken-wings-and-beer night at some alternate United Nations. Ford had one sublime virtue which all politicians should study and imitate. He did not think he was better than the people who voted for him. He didn't prate about respecting the voters; he actually did it. Some people like to say he anticipated the politics of Donald Trump. Not so. He was more Ralph Klein, another wild politician whose heart had more intelligence than the brains who looked down upon him. And whose style and manner kept more believing in his politics than 50 Senates full of the distinguished, the sophisticated, the eminent and the connected.

Rob Ford, for all the controversy, kept the line open with the common man. In the words of the same Lincoln, Mr. Ford was "of the people, by the people, for the people," with a vengeance. It's very sad to see this decent man so wonderfully gifted emotionally, and likewise so burdened, die in mid-life before we knew the all of him.[5]

MIKE DEL GRANDE

Rob Ford was fiercely loyal. In return, he would test for loyalty—you do not just earn it. Every day for two years, at eight in the morning, I would meet with Rob's office team. No other councillor, not even the deputy mayor, participated to this extent. I knew if I was taken into his confidence, there was nothing he wouldn't do for me. I remember when I was first hospitalized, Rob came to visit me in the hospital. I was in a semi-private room. Rob kept insisting with hospital staff that I should be in a private room and he would pay for it. Rob has been vilified, but people are not aware of the kind and generous gestures he has always provided for his buddies.

GAVIN TIGHE

In the interest of full disclosure, I was Rob and Doug Ford's lawyer and continue to be. My comments are obviously and admittedly biased.

I recall my then very young nephew commenting when someone mentioned my retainer at the height of Rob and Doug's legal battles, saying, "Wow, you must be really busy."

Rob Ford certainly had far more than his fair share of legal skirmishes during his tenure at city hall.

There is definitely a political (buttressed by media) establishment in Toronto, Ontario and Canada. As with any establishment, it works for those in the establishment. No one who benefits from an establishment really likes anyone who rocks the boat. That was certainly true for Rob. He had been an outsider and contrarian on city council for years, but when a wave of popular support for the "un-politician" swept Rob, as mayor, into office, the establishment would not go quietly.

And in this quest, the courts were just another arena to attack and distract him.

Admittedly, Rob often made it easy. His "say whatever's on your mind" style made him popular with his base of ordinary people who were sick of typical politicians reading teleprompters with canned photo-op speeches polished by teams of handlers and lawyers, but caused others in a political cul-

ture that has become intolerant to anything but "political correctness" to cringe. While in some respects, many found Rob's style refreshing, it also made him an easy target . . . Rob certainly had his own personal demons, which the media, seemingly almost gleefully, put on full display. Whether Rob's personal problems were caused or seriously aggravated by the incredible strain of being under constant attack is hard to say. Certainly, no elected official in Toronto has ever endured the relentless pursuit that Rob did in the legal, political and personal arenas.

One thing for sure, Rob was a heck of a witness in a courtroom, and during the five-day trial in the defence of a defamation action in 2012, he calmly sat in the courtroom and gave forthright testimony in front of the crowded court, filled with members of the public and often openly hostile media. If Rob had any personal problems, none were on display in the witness box during that trial.

Despite the personal problems that would later be revealed about Rob, at the end of the day, he took a simple message of respecting taxpayers that resonated and continues to resonate to city hall and beyond, and that simple message shook up the establishment.

While Rob Ford definitely paid the price for his forthright and brash style, he didn't spend the taxpayers' money doing it. In my opinion, this is precisely why the establishment, particularly the backroom political establishment, was so adverse to him from the outset. Rob Ford's enduring popularity continues to confound this same establishment. As Rob was fond of saying, he was not perfect. But then again, who is? Ordinary people related to Rob's imperfections. He was one of them and, from their perspective, he stood up for them. Perhaps that is something the establishment will never really understand.

CHAPTER 24

Looking Forward

Rob may be gone, but Ford Nation remains. And Ford Nation is not about political parties, conservative or liberal allegiances, personal beliefs, or whether someone is wealthy or not. Ford Nation is about standing up to the political elite; the same old, same old; wasted money; and unaccountable and unreachable leadership. Rob knew what this is all about; the question for the rest of us is what comes next. As we think about the future, here are some remarks from my sister-in-law, my mother and my nephew.

RENATA FORD

Looking back, I know what Rob did as mayor was right. Even through all the criticism from the media and everything, what he did was right. Rob was the people's mayor, and that's the way I think every politician should be. It's not about the way they look, how they talk or how they dress. It's about what's right for the people. That kind of work needs to continue on. In what way—or who will do it—I have no idea.

It's still so hard for us. Rob died less than a year ago, so it's a huge adjustment for me and the kids. But he taught them to work hard and do the best job they can and always give it their all. Those are lessons they'll never forget. Both kids talk about going into politics someday, and I will support them no matter what they do, but for now, their education is my number one priority. I'm very proud of them.

DIANE FORD

I'd like to see Doug stay in business, but I wouldn't talk him out of politics, and I'd be behind him 100 percent. Would I like it? No. Maybe I shouldn't say that, but being in politics and being in public life are very hard.

There were days that I was held hostage in my home. I couldn't go out because there were so many media people surrounding the property. The media are not like that to every family, but every family isn't the Ford family. It was cruel.

As for Michael, he's different than the other boys. He'll carry on Rob's legacy, but he has a different approach. He's a much gentler person. He weighs things all the time. He sees both sides of it, and he really weighs it.

I do worry more, but I'm also hopeful about the future. The most important thing is health, more so than money. Money isn't any good if you haven't got health. If you have health, you've got happiness, and I think we do have happiness. It comes in fragments every once in a while, but it's there.

MICHAEL FORD

Rob helped me understand that politics is one of the best pathways to create a difference in society, depending on what difference you want to create, whether that's in a city, in a town, in a community. A city council in particular has that direct impact. Because everything a municipal councillor deals with affects people's day-to-day lives. There are tangible things, stuff that people use. Provincial and federal governments definitely affect people's lives too, but at a higher level, whereas a city has transit, police, fire, garbage pickup—all those kinds of things.

Right now, my focus is crime reduction. Crime in general is on a decline in Toronto, but shootings are on a drastic increase. When we talk about crime, it encompasses a lot more than just breaking the law. Crime is directly related to people's education, their socio-economic status, and poverty, and it's a vicious cycle. That's one thing Rob helped me understand. So I think we need to break the cycle of poverty. That's very important. A community needs investment. People need good jobs, not just jobs that pay, but jobs that people want to do. I want to start a community centre in Etobicoke North—Rob's old ward—because there's a huge demand for a community centre.

Rob absolutely left me a legacy to take on. That legacy, I think, is about serving the people. I think Rob always remembered that. Whether people agreed or disagreed with him, he cared. I think everyone agrees with that. He cared about his constituents, he cared about the city, and he cared about his job. That's the part of his legacy that really speaks to me today. One of the trademark points is customer service—something Rob championed and branded. That's what I think it's all about. Do all politicians do that? No, they don't. In my short time as an elected representative, I've seen that already. Rob knew it all too well.

In my time as a councillor, I've learned that you have policy governing a city. Policy is words in black and white on sheets of paper that say how the city is supposed to be run. But a councillor adds (or should add) the human aspect of it, because all those policies do not represent people in every case and don't always best serve them. So it's up to the councillor to say, "Hey, that bylaw is not helping this particular person act, so how do we make this work?"

As for me, my political future is not finished. There are things I want to do and ways I want to be involved with the future of this country. In the meantime, I believe that those of us who believe in Ford Nation will go on to serve the people at all different levels. Even now, people call us for absolutely everything, even stuff that we can't deal with, so we always try to point them in the right direction. Whether it's a federal issue, provincial or municipal, when average people need help and aren't getting answers, they call us, and we call them back. In this regard, I want to carry on Rob's legacy.

When Rob ran for mayor, we realized Ford Nation had become its own strategic voting block, even though we hadn't really planned that. Ford Nation, I believe, could quite possibly be the biggest block in Canada outside of any political party. There are roughly 340,000 people in Ford Nation; that's just in Toronto and doesn't count the hundreds of thousands of supporters throughout the 905, 705 and 519 area codes—not to mention the rest of the country. They stuck by Rob through the worst of the worst times, because they all knew he was sticking by them in city hall. He would've stuck by them all the way to the top too, if only he'd had the chance.

There are a lot of haters out there. I know that. There are people who have attacked our family in many different ways. But I believe that most of those haters never sat down and talked to us, got to know us or tried to understand where we were coming from. But whenever we had a chance to talk to those folks, many of them said the same thing: "You guys are nothing like the media portrays you." So I would say, before you judge people in life, you should first sit down and talk to them. You might find a human being, someone with a family, someone with a dedication to public service. Someone like Rob Ford.

In terms of final words, I'm turning to one last tribute. Here is my niece, Stephanie—Rob's daughter—whose remarks about her dad in her eulogy were the best anyone could ever say:

STEPHANIE FORD

Thank you so much for being here today. It means so much to my brother, Dougie, and I. My dad was a great mayor. He helped a lot of people. He was also [an] amazing dad. He was so happy whenever he was with us, and he was so nice to us, but also strict sometimes, like a dad should be. He would buy us the best toys and take us to amazing places, but what matters was that we were happy together. I remember at the hospital, he smiled at me and he said, "Stephanie, I might not be here for too much longer." He said, "I want you to remember that I'll always love you. I need you and your brother to be strong for your mom." I know my dad is in a better place now. And he's the mayor of heaven now. Dougie and I know that he will be with us forever. I love him so much, and I want to thank everyone again for all your support. Thank you so much.

ENDNOTES

Chapter 1: The Most Misunderstood Mayor in the World

1. Rob Ford, interview by Bill Carroll, *The Bill Carroll Show*, Talk Radio AM640, October 1, 2015, http://www.640toronto.com/2015/10/01/carroll-rob-ford-returns-to-the-bill-carroll-show/.
2. *National Post*, "Don Cherry's Speech at Rob Ford's Inauguration," NationalPost.com, December 7, 2010, http://news.nationalpost.com/full-comment/don-cherrys-speech-at-rob-fords-inauguration.
3. David Rider, "Don Cherry Rips 'Left-wing Pinkos' at Council Inaugural," TheStar.com, December 7, 2010, https://www.thestar.com/news/city_hall/2010/12/07/don_cherry_rips_leftwing_pinkos_at_council_inaugural.html.
4. Rob Ford, interview by Bill Carroll, *The Bill Carroll Show*, Talk Radio AM640, October 1, 2015, http://www.640toronto.com/2015/10/01/carroll-rob-ford-returns-to-the-bill-carroll-show/.
5. Ibid.

Chapter 2: The Ford Family

1. Mike Harris, Mike Harris, eulogy at Rob Ford's funeral, March 30, 2016.

Chapter 8: A Man of the People

1. Bill Lankhof, "Welcome to Loserville," TorontoSun.com, last modified November 1, 2009, http://www.torontosun.com/sports/columnists/bill_lankhof/2009/11/01/11594956-sun.html.

Chapter 10: Second Term

1. Marlene Leung, "'A Profoundly Human Guy': Rob Ford Honoured by Colleagues, Friends," CTVnews.ca, last modified March 22, 2016, http://www.ctvnews.ca/canada/a-profoundly-human-guy-rob-ford-honoured-by-colleagues-friends-1.2827571.
2. Royson James, "How City Hall Rewards Thrift," TheStar.com, May 2, 2007, https://www.thestar.com/opinion/columnists/2007/05/02/how_city_hall_rewards_thrift.html.
3. Vanessa Lu, "City Council Cracks Down on Expenses," TheStar.com, July 17, 2008, https://www.thestar.com/news/gta/2008/07/17/city_council_cracks_down_on_expenses.html.
4. Marcus Gee, "How Toronto's Golden Boy Lost His Shine," TheGlobeandMail.com, last modified September 6, 2012, http://www.theglobeandmail.com/news/toronto/how-torontos-golden-boy-lost-his-shine/article790536/.

Chapter 11: Doug

1. Patrick White, "Doug Ford: Riding Shotgun in the Fordmobile," The Globe and Mail.com, last modified August 24, 2012, http://www.theglobeandmail.com/news/toronto/doug-ford-riding-shotgun-in-the-fordmobile/article1322412/.

Chapter 13: The Once and Future Mayor

1. Kelly Grant, John Lorinc and Anna Mehler Paperny, "Ford's Dominant Victory Ushers in a New Era for Toronto," TheGlobeandMail.com, last modified August 23, 2012, http://www.theglobeandmail.com/news/toronto/fords-dominant-victory-ushers-in-a-new-era-for-toronto/article1215551/.
2. CBC News, "Opposition Calls for Smitherman's Head," CBC.ca, last modified October 7, 2009, http://www.cbc.ca/news/canada/toronto/opposition-calls-for-smitherman-s-head-1.834387.
3. Linda Diebel, "Adam Giambrone Says Sorry for Relationship with Young Woman," TheStar.com, February 9, 2010, https://www.thestar.com/news/city_hall/2010/02/09/adam_giambrone_says_sorry_for_relationship_with_young_woman.html.

4. Kelly Grant, "Former Student Football Player Says Rob Ford Never Hit Him," TheGlobeandMail.com, last modified August 23, 2012, http://www.theglobeandmail.com/news/toronto/former-student-football-player-says-rob-ford-never-hit-him/article1212647/.
5. David Rider, "Giorgio Mammoliti Quits Mayoral Race," TheStar.com, July 5, 2010, https://www.thestar.com/news/city_hall/2010/07/05/giorgio_mammoliti_quits_mayoral_race.html.
6. Cory Ruf, "Ford Says No to Debate, So Smitherman Cries Fowl," NationalPost.com, July 28, 2010, http://news.nationalpost.com/posted-toronto/ford-says-no-to-debate-so-smitherman-camps-cries-fowl.

Chapter 14: Last Stop: Gravy Train

1. Natalie Alcoba, "Toronto Council Rides with Stintz on Transit," NationalPost.com, February 8, 2012, http://news.nationalpost.com/posted-toronto/future-of-transit-expansion-in-toronto-comes-to-a-head-wednesday.
2. CBC News, "TTC Essential Service Legislation Passes," CBC.ca, last modified March 30, 2011, http://www.cbc.ca/news/canada/toronto/ttc-essential-service-legislation-passes-1.1043311.
3. Andrew Barr, "Graphic; The TTC Fare Hike, and Fares Over the Years," NationalPost.com, December 15, 2011, http://news.nationalpost.com/posted-toronto/graphic-the-ttc-fare-hike-and-fares-over-the-years.
4. CBC News, "Toronto Has Saved $11.9M through Private Garbage Pickup," CBC.ca, last modified December 16, 2013, http://www.cbc.ca/news/canada/toronto/toronto-has-saved-11-9m-through-private-garbage-pickup-1.2466736.
5. Tess Kalinowski, "High Stakes in Streetcar Game," TheStar.com, June 10, 2009, https://www.thestar.com/news/gta/2009/06/10/high_stakes_in_streetcar_game.html.
6. Jerry Agar, "St.Clair Going Off the Rails Again," TorontoSun.com, last modified June 17, 2016, http://www.torontosun.com/2016/06/17/st-clair-going-off-the-rails-again.
7. Bryn Weese, "TTC Defends Sole-Source Contract," Transit.Toronto.on.ca, last modified September 25, 2009, http://transit.toronto.on.ca/archives/data/200909250429.shtml.

8. Natalie Alcoba, "Police Board Still Asking for 10% Cut, but Allows for It to Be Spread over Two Years," NationalPost.com, October 5, 2011, http://news.nationalpost.com/posted-toronto/police-board-still-asking-for-10-cut-but-allows-for-it-to-be-spread-over-two-years.
9. Alyshah Hasham, "Rob Ford Avoids Ticket for Talking on Cellphone and Driving," TheStar.com, July 27, 2011, https://www.thestar.com/news/gta/2011/07/27/rob_ford_avoids_ticket_for_talking_on_cellphone_and_driving.html.
10. Daniel Dale, "What Does Rob Ford Do All Day?" TheStar.com, March 24, 2011, https://www.thestar.com/news/city_hall/2011/03/24/what_does_rob_ford_do_all_day.html.
11. Adrian Morrow, "Man Charged with Death Threat against Toronto Mayor Rob Ford," TheGlobeandMail.com, last modified August 10, 2011, http://www.theglobeandmail.com/news/toronto/man-charged-with-death-threat-against-toronto-mayor-rob-ford/article589957/.
12. Michael Woods, "Toronto Mayor Had No Time for This Hour Has 22 Minutes," TheStar.com, October 25, 2011, https://www.thestar.com/news/gta/2011/10/25/toronto_mayor_had_no_time_for_this_hour_has_22_minutes.html.

Chapter 15: Selling Toronto to the World

1. "The City with Josh Matlow on Newstalk 1010," JoshMatlow.ca, http://joshmatlow.ca/media/the-city-with-josh-matlow-on-newstalk-1010.html.
2. Allison Cross, "Thorn in His Side: The Ongoing Feud between Adam Vaughan and Rob Ford," NationalPost.com, September 11, 2012, http://news.nationalpost.com/posted-toronto/thorn-in-his-side-the-ongoing-feud-between-adam-vaughan-and-rob-ford.

Chapter 17: Under Fire

1. Rob Ford, interview by Bill Carroll, *The Bill Carroll Show*, Talk Radio AM640, October 1, 2015, http://www.640toronto.com/2015/10/01/carroll-rob-ford-returns-to-the-bill-carroll-show/.

2. Robyn Doolittle and Kevin Donovan, "Rob Ford in 'Crack Cocaine' Video Scandal," TheStar.com, May 16, 2013, https://www.thestar.com/news/city_hall/2013/05/16/toronto_mayor_rob_ford_in_crack_cocaine_video_scandal.html.
3. Rob Ford, interview by Bill Carroll.
4. CBC News, "Toronto's Rob Ford Calls Groping Claim 'Completely False,'" CBC.ca, last modified March 8, 2013, http://www.cbc.ca/news/canada/toronto/toronto-s-rob-ford-calls-groping-claim-completely-false-1.1305579.

Chapter 18: Roller Coaster Ride

1. CBC News, "Toronto Mayor Rob Ford Denies Crack Cocaine Allegations," CBC.ca, last modified May 17, 2013, http://www.cbc.ca/news/canada/toronto/toronto-mayor-rob-ford-denies-crack-cocaine-allegations-1.1302821.
2. Rob Ford, interview by Bill Carroll, *The Bill Carroll Show*, Talk Radio AM640, October 1, 2015, http://www.640toronto.com/2015/10/01/carroll-rob-ford-returns-to-the-bill-carroll-show/.
3. TheStar.com, "Rob Ford Crack Scandal: Transcript of Doug Ford's Statement," TheStar.com, May 22, 2013, https://www.thestar.com/news/gta/2013/05/22/rob_ford_crack_scandal_transcript_of_doug_fords_statement.html.
4. Rob Ford, interview by David "Menzoid" Menzies, *Menzoid Mornings*, TorontoSun.com, March 1, 2013, http://www.torontosun.com/videos/editors-picks/featured-tor/1213592864001/pigskin-and-politics/2196803502001.
5. Daniel Dale, "Catholic School Board Investigating Rob Ford's 'Inaccurate' Sun News Interview," TheStar.com, March 7, 2013, https://www.thestar.com/news/city_hall/2013/03/07/catholic_school_board_investigating_rob_fords_inaccurate_sun_news_interview.html.
6. Sarah Boesveld, Adrian Humphreys, Jake Edmiston and Peter Kuitenbrouwer, "Rob Ford Court Documents Reveal Staffers Thought Prostitute Was in His Office, Mayor Was Driving Drunk," NationalPost.com, November 13, 2013, http://news.nationalpost.com/toronto/rob-ford-court-documents-reveal-staffers-thought-prostitute-was-in-his-office-mayor-was-driving-drunk.

7. Sandie Benitah and Chris Fox, "Ford Responds after Two More Staffers Quit," CP24.com, last modified May 30, 2013, http://www.cp24.com/news/ford-responds-after-two-more-staffers-quit-1.1303368.
8. Christie Blatchford, "Christie Blatchford: Toronto Police in Delicate Dance Over Alleged Rob Ford Link to Drug Raids," NationalPost.com, June 13, 2013, http://news.nationalpost.com/full-comment/christie-blatchford-toronto-police-in-delicate-dance-over-alleged-rob-ford-link-to-drug-raids.
9. Michele Mandel, "Court Asks for Second Look at G20 Complaint Against Police Chief Bill Blair," TorontoSun.com, last modified June 7, 2013, http://www.torontosun.com/2013/06/07/court-asks-for-second-look-at-g20-complaint-against-police-chief-bill-blair.
10. Chris Doucette, "Police Chief Bill Blair Vows Answers in TTC Shooting of Sammy Yatim," TorontoSun.com, last modified July 29, 2013, http://www.torontosun.com/2013/07/29/police-chief-bill-blair-comments-on-fatal-ttc-streetcar-shooting.
11. Patrick White and Karen Howlett, "Doug Ford's Broadside at Police Board Member Seen as Calculated Strike on a Tory Ally," TheGlobeandMail.com, last modified November 5, 2013, http://www.theglobeandmail.com/news/toronto/police-board-member-andy-pringle-dismisses-ford-allegation-that-he-is-in-conflict-of-interest/article15272759/.
12. Marlene Leung, "CTV Poll: Torontonians Evenly Split in Their Belief of Rob Ford Crack Allegations," CTVNews.ca, last modified June 1, 2013, http://www.ctvnews.ca/canada/ctv-poll-torontonians-evenly-split-in-their-belief-of-rob-ford-crack-allegations-1.1306986.
13. The Canadian Press, "Rob Ford Crack Stories Subject of Press Council Complaints," CBC.ca, last modified August 20, 2013, http://www.cbc.ca/news/canada/toronto/rob-ford-crack-stories-subject-of-press-council-complaints-1.1384936.
14. CBC News, "Star and Globe Defend Their Rob and Doug Ford Stories," CBC.ca, last modified September 9, 2013, http://www.cbc.ca/news/canada/toronto/star-and-globe-defend-their-rob-and-doug-ford-stories-1.1699053.

15. "Rob Ford: The Good, the Bad, and the Ugly," TorontoSun.com, August 17, 2013, http://www.torontosun.com/2013/08/16/rob-ford-the-good-the-bad-and-the-ugly.
16. Don Peat, "Rob Ford Tours TCHC Building, Promises Repairs," TorontoSun.com, last modified September 18, 2013, http://www.torontosun.com/2013/09/18/rob-ford-tours-tchc-building-promises-repairs.
17. The Canadian Press, "Expense Claims from Pan Am Games Execs under Fire," CBC.ca, last modified September 30, 2013, http://www.cbc.ca/news/canada/toronto/expense-claims-from-pan-am-games-execs-under-fire-1.1874042.
18. Megan O'Toole, "Rob Ford Right to Criticize Expense Claims by Pan Am Games Executives: David Peterson," NationalPost.com, October 29, 2013, http://news.nationalpost.com/toronto/rob-ford-right-to-criticize-expense-claims-by-pan-am-games-executives-david-peterson.
19. Joshua Freeman, "Ford Touts Record after Stintz Says She'll Run for Mayor in 2014," CP24.com, last modified October 28, 2013, http://www.cp24.com/news/ford-touts-record-after-stintz-says-she-ll-run-for-mayor-in-2014-1.1515977.
20. CBC News, "Police Chief Bill Blair on the Rob Ford Video," CBC.ca, last modified October 31, 2013, http://www.cbc.ca/news/canada/toronto/police-chief-bill-blair-on-the-rob-ford-video-1.2303505.
21. Joe Warmington, "Blair May Have Overstepped His Authority: Senator," TorontoSun.com, last modified November 5, 2013, http://www.torontosun.com/2013/11/04/blair-may-have-overstepped-his-authority-senator.
22. Ibid.
23. "Doug Ford Calls on Police Chief to Step Down," CBC Player video, CBC.ca, 8:17, November 5, 2013, http://www.cbc.ca/player/play/2416049183.

Chapter 19: Late-Breaking News

1. "Full Transcript of Mayor Rob Ford Admitting He Smoked Crack Cocaine," TheStar.com, November 5, 2013, https://www.thestar.com/news/city_hall/2013/11/05/full_transcript_of_mayor_rob_ford_admitting_he_smoked_crack_cocaine.html.

2. Joe Warmington, "'I Need F—in 10 Minutes to Make Sure He's Dead': New Rob Ford Video Surfaces," TorontoSun.com, last modified November 7, 2013, http://www.torontosun.com/2013/11/07/i-need-f---in-10-minutes-to-make-sure-hes-dead-new-rob-ford-video-surfaces.
3. Sandie Benitah, "Ford's Mother 'Heartbroken' over Controversy Surrounding Mayor," CP24.com, November 7, 2013, http://www.cp24.com/news/ford/ford-s-mother-heartbroken-over-controversy-surrounding-mayor-1.1532938.
4. Rob Ford, interview by Bill Carroll, *The Bill Carroll Show*, Talk Radio AM640, October 1, 2015, http://www.640toronto.com/2015/10/01/carroll-rob-ford-returns-to-the-bill-carroll-show/.
5. CBC News, "Rob Ford Admits Buying Drugs, Council Urges Him to Take Leave," CBC.ca, last modified November 13, 2013, http://www.cbc.ca/news/canada/toronto/rob-ford-admits-buying-drugs-council-urges-him-to-take-leave-1.2424106.
6. Lee-Anne Goodman, "Tory MP Kenney Breaks Ranks, Calls for Rob Ford to Resign," GlobalNews.ca, November 19, 2013, http://globalnews.ca/news/977696/tory-mp-kenney-breaks-ranks-calls-for-rob-ford-to-resign/.
7. Ibid.

Chapter 20: Infamy

1. Maryam Shah, "Mayor Rob Ford Cheered at Etobicoke Santa Claus Parade," TorontoSun.com, last modified December 7, 2013, http://www.torontosun.com/2013/12/07/mayor-rob-ford-cheered-at-etobicoke-santa-claus-parade.
2. Rob Ford, interview by Peter Mansbridge, CBC News, November 18, 2013, http://www.cbc.ca/news/canada/toronto/rob-ford-says-he-s-quit-drinking-has-had-come-to-jesus-moment-1.2430801.
3. Doug Ford, interview by Peter Mansbridge, CBC News, November 18, 2013, http://www.cbc.ca/news/canada/toronto/rob-ford-says-he-s-quit-drinking-has-had-come-to-jesus-moment-1.2430801.
4. Rob Ford, interview by Conrad Black, *The Zoomer*, December 9, 2013, http://www.torontosun.com/2013/12/09/ive-got-no-problem-doing-a-drug-test-mayor-rob-ford-to-conrad-black.

5. Antonella Artuso, "Deputy Mayor Norm Kelly Apologizes for Florida Trip during Hydro Outage," TorontoSun.com, last modified December 27, 2013, http://www.torontosun.com/2013/12/27/deputy-mayor-norm-kelly-goes-to-florida-amid-hydro-outage-crisis.
6. Jenny Yuen, "Mayor Rob Ford on Ice Storm Recovery: 'We Have Made Progress,'" TorontoSun.com, last modified December 26, 2013, http://www.torontosun.com/2013/12/25/mayor-rob-ford-on-ice-storm-recovery-we-have-made-progress.
7. Artuso, "Deputy Mayor Norm Kelly Apologizes for Florida Trip during Hydro Outage."
8. Don Peat, "Ice Storm Response Thaws Mayor Rob Ford's Approval Rating: Poll," TorontoSun.com, last modified January 8, 2014, http://www.torontosun.com/2014/01/08/ice-storm-response-thaws-mayor-rob-fords-approval-rating-poll.
9. Chris Jones, "Rob Ford Was a Complicated Man," Esquire.com, February 14, 2014, http://www.esquire.com/news-politics/interviews/a23742/rob-ford-interview-0314/.
10. Ibid.
11. Rob Ford, interview by Jimmy Kimmel, *Jimmy Kimmel Live*, March 3, 2014, https://www.youtube.com/watch?v=MIMckkviH-s.
12. Jimmy Kimmel, interview by Jimmy Kimmel, *Jimmy Kimmel Live*, March 3, 2014, https://www.youtube.com/watch?v=MIMckkviH-s.
13. Matt Kwong, "How Toronto Mayor Rob Ford Could Win Again," CBC.ca, last modified April 18, 2014, http://www.cbc.ca/news/canada/toronto/how-toronto-mayor-rob-ford-could-win-again-1.2614581.
14. Forum Research Inc., "Chow Is Still on Top in Mayoral Sweeps," press release, April 15, 2014, http://www.forumresearch.com/forms/News%20Archives/News%20Releases/42134_TO_Approval_Horserace_News_Release_(2014.04.15)_Forum_Research.pdf.
15. Robyn Doolittle and Greg McArthur, "Rob Ford Takes Leave as Recent Drug Videos Emerge," TheGlobeandMail.com, last modified May 1, 2014, http://www.theglobeandmail.com/news/toronto/rob-ford-takes-leave-as-new-drug-video-emerges/article18354671/.
16. Ibid.

Chapter 21: Getting Help

1. Rob Ford, interview by Bill Carroll, *The Bill Carroll Show*, Talk Radio AM640, October 1, 2015, http://www.640toronto.com/2015/10/01/carroll-rob-ford-returns-to-the-bill-carroll-show/.
2. Ibid.
3. Anne Kingston and Charlie Gillis, "Why Rob Ford Isn't Done Yet," Macleans.ca, May 13, 2014, http://www.macleans.ca/news/canada/why-rob-ford-isnt-done-yet/.
4. Joe Warmington, "'Rehab Is Amazing': Rob Ford Speaks to Sun," TorontoSun.com, last modified May 7, 2014, http://www.torontosun.com/2014/05/07/rehab-is-amazing-rob-ford-speaks-to-sun.
5. Don Peat, "Chow, DoFo Want Shorter Municipal Campaign Period," TorontoSun.com, last modified June 10, 2014, http://www.torontosun.com/2014/06/10/olivia-chow-vows-to-shorten-campaign-period.
6. Ibid.
7. Warmington, "'Rehab Is Amazing': Rob Ford Speaks to Sun."
8. Rob Ford, interview by Dwight Drummond, CBC News, July 2, 2014, https://www.youtube.com/watch?v=Po7-r6wR0FI.
9. Ibid.
10. Rob Ford, interview by Bill Carroll.
11. Elizabeth Church, "Gridlock Woes Push Tory to Top of Toronto's Mayoral Race," TheGlobeandMail.com, last modified September 3, 2014, http://www.theglobeandmail.com/news/toronto/tory-takes-14-point-lead-over-ford-in-new-globe-poll/article20312607/.
12. Natalie Alcoba, "Karen Stintz Drops Out of Toronto Mayoral Race, Sets Sights on Becoming Next CFL Commissioner," NationalPost.com, August 20, 2014, http://news.nationalpost.com/toronto/is-karen-stintz-dropping-out-of-toronto-mayoral-race-campaign-team-has-no-comment-about-speculation.

Chapter 22: The Diagnosis

1. Rob Ford, interview by Bill Carroll, *The Bill Carroll Show,* Talk Radio AM640, October 1, 2015, http://www.640toronto.com/2015/10/01/carroll-rob-ford-returns-to-the-bill-carroll-show/.

2. Jordan Chittley, “Rob Ford Hospitalized: ‘Working Diagnosis’ Is Tumour,” CTVNews.ca, last modified September 10, 2014, http://toronto.ctvnews.ca/rob-ford-hospitalized-working-diagnosis-is-tumour-1.2001382.
3. Lauren Pelley, “Rob Ford’s Diagnosis: What Is a Pleomorphic Liposarcoma?” TheStar.com, September 17, 2014, https://www.thestar.com/news/gta/2014/09/17/rob_fords_diagnosis_what_is_a_pleomorphic_liposarcoma.html.
4. CBC News, “Rob Ford Statement: Mayor Withdraws from Race,” CBC.ca, last modified September 12, 2014, http://www.cbc.ca/news/canada/toronto/rob-ford-statement-mayor-withdraws-from-race-1.2764685.
5. Ann Hui, Elizabeth Church and Fred Lum, “Rob Ford Drops Out of Mayoral Race, Doug Ford Running in His Place,” TheGlobeandMail.com, last modified September 12, 2014, http://www.theglobeandmail.com/news/toronto/ford-dropping-out-of-toronto-mayoral-race/article20576741/.
6. Elizabeth Church and Ann Hui, “Doug Ford Running for Mayor Was Long-time Back-up Plan: Sources,” TheGlobeandMail.com, last modified September 13, 2014, http://www.theglobeandmail.com/news/toronto/passing-the-political-torch-from-one-ford-brother-to-the-other/article20592615/.
7. Ibid.
8. “‘Some Nights I Cry Myself to Sleep’—Rob Ford on Cancer and Treatment,” YouTube video, 2:11, posted by *The Globe and Mail*, October 2, 2014, https://www.youtube.com/watch?v=NN88GS_AXsY.

Chapter 23: Saying Goodbye

1. Rob Ford, interview by Bill Carroll, *The Bill Carroll Show*, Talk Radio AM640, October 1, 2015, http://www.640toronto.com/2015/10/01/carroll-rob-ford-returns-to-the-bill-carroll-show/.
2. Ibid.
3. Joe Warmington, “Rob Ford: ‘I Am on My Way Back,’” TorontoSun.com, last modified January 3, 2016, http://www.torontosun.com/2016/01/03/rob-ford-i-am-on-my-way-back.

4. "A Transcript of the Eulogies at Rob Ford's Funeral Service," Macleans.ca, March 30, 2016, http://www.macleans.ca/news/canada/hes-the-mayor-of-heaven-now-a-transcript-of-rob-ford-tributes/.
5. Rex Murphy, "Remembering Rob Ford," *The National*, video, 3:10, http://www.cbc.ca/news/thenational/rex-murphy-remembering-rob-ford-1.3505127.